TICKET TO
LATVIA

TICKET TO
LATVIA

A Journey from Berlin
to the Baltic

MARCUS TANNER

Henry Holt and Company
New York

Library of Congress Cataloging-in-Publication Data
Tanner, Marcus.
Ticket to Latvia : a journey from Berlin to the Baltic / Marcus
Tanner.—1st American ed.
p.   cm.
ISBN 0-8050-1346-6
1. Europe, Eastern—Description and travel. 2. Tanner, Marcus—
Journeys—Europe, Eastern. I. Title.
DJK18.T36   1990
914.7—dc20   90-32926
                                                        CIP

First American Edition

CONTENTS

Contents

PROLOGUE

THE SUN was shining over the Elbe. Dresden relaxed, like a former beauty who feels more comfortable in soft lighting than under the harsh scrutiny of midday. I was eating an ice cream and sitting opposite the Opera House clutching a brochure entitled 'Welcome to the Florence of the Elbe'. It was full of the windy trumpeting I had come to expect of the East German tourist authority. 'Some Florence,' I murmured to myself, 'even the city centre has not been rebuilt forty years after the war.'

My eye fell on a very refined-looking lady standing outside the Opera House, holding a small clutch-bag. She stood waiting for a taxi with perfect Prussian poise and a slightly tragic air.

I imagined her forty years ago as a little girl with short blonde hair held back by a tortoiseshell comb, in the East Prussian town where she lived. She is playing listlessly on the parquet floor of the hallway of a dark apartment decorated with faded nicotine-coloured wallpaper. Her mother, a tall gaunt version of her daughter, with blonde hair cut in a bob like Magda Goebbels and dark rings under her eyes from a succession of sleepless nights, is standing by the telephone, smoking nervously. The radio blares in the kitchen.

The Russian army is advancing through East Prussia towards Berlin. This army will avenge the siege of Leningrad.

She telephones Berlin for information about her husband. She has no idea what to do. She does not yet realise that he died several weeks before.

Now she is running down the platform of the local railway station. The station is in chaos. Everyone is abandoning their homes before the Russians arrive. The little girl cries beause she drops her doll and it is immediately lost in the crowd. She is bundled on to the train by her mother whom she does not see again. Years later in Dresden she thinks over this incident, trying hard to remember each detail of this parting, but in the passage of time her mother's features have blurred.

My reverie is interrupted by the screech of tyres. A hot little bus with steamed-up windows has stopped outside the Opera House. There is the sound of shouting. The doors are flung open and out spills a buzzing crowd of short people with gold teeth. The men look ill at ease in nylon suits which are too tight. Their necks bulge out of their shirt collars.

Peasants in suits! They are Russians. The victors. A malicious thought comes into my head. 'The vandals are sight-seeing in Rome.' I ask the bus driver where they have come from.

'Leningrad.'

As the Russians stand blinking into the sunset and murmuring appreciatively about the Opera House I wonder how they feel about the land they are in, a land whose people inflicted immense suffering upon them, but of which they are now in a sense the masters. Exultant? Fearful? And how do the Prussians and Saxons of East Germany feel about them? I look round to catch the expression on the face of the very refined woman of Dresden. There is no one there. She has disappeared into a taxi.

TICKET TO
LATVIA

BERLIN

On the banks of the Spree

... a German town in Brandenburg March. It is large,
beautiful and well built. The palace of the Prince,
various large squares, regular houses and fine modern
streets make the town pleasant.

Le Grand Dictionnaire Historique, 1687

BEYOND A SIGN that read 'You are now leaving the American sector'
was an empty square illuminated by a spotlight. It resembled an empty
stage between scenes. The soldier at Checkpoint Charlie was provoca-
tively officious. He insisted on opening both my camera and my
tube of toothpaste.

As the soldier moved slowly through my belongings, fingering
each and every one of my possessions with long, probing fingers,
like a doctor examining the internal organs of his patient, I felt the
presence of the wall behind him with a physical longing.

Three letters made me want to visit East Germany; three infectious
letters: DDR, pronounced Day-Day-Err. No country which defined
itself in three letters, I decided, could be bad. They sounded chatty
and municipal and vaguely didactic; like BBC or NHS.

What lay behind the Berlin Wall drew me as much as the structure
of the wall itself repelled me. The previous day I had walked the
length of it on the western side. As I did so, I imagined holding
a glass to the grey and concrete stones to catch a million muffled
whispers on the other side.

The electric door clicked open. A switch had been pressed by unseen hands. At last I was in the secret garden! The Berlin Wall may have been built to keep the East Germans in, but as far as I was concerned, it existed to keep me out.

I entered the no-man's land on the eastern side of the wall. Standing under the spotlight I looked back at the mass of grey stone and barbed wire. To the east lay the stately dome of Berlin cathedral. Beyond were the lights of the Alexander Square with its needle-shaped radio tower. Behind me on the other side of the wall lay the west.

Was that it? Having penetrated its mystery, the wall was already reduced in stature in my eyes. There was no secret garden after all; just another part of the city I had already been in. Over the next few months I pushed east from Berlin through Poland and the Baltic to Leningrad. I still remembered the metal gate with its innocent-sounding click.

Berlin is a modern city by European standards; a mere hamlet when it first peeps shyly around the door of known history around the year 1240. There are cities like Cracow and Prague which wear their history on their sleeves and call to those who will listen about their lost days of glory. Berlin does not belong to that school. A clutch of undistinguished medieval churches, marooned and embarrassed by their humble origins, stand amid the raw concrete of the Alexander Square. They are all that remains of two villages named Berlin and Kölln which sprang up seven and a half centuries ago on the banks of the river Spree.

Berlin has suffered. It shows its pain in cracks and stretchmarks that are perceived rather than seen. There is a princely boulevard named the Unter den Linden; but it ends rather appropriately in a chaotic snarl of barbed wire. The Berliners accept this philosophically. On Sundays they stroll purposefully up the Unter den Linden, gaze blankly into the no-man's land of the Pariser Square, and then walk back again.

There is a stretch of riverbank in Berlin where a block of flats in the east overlooks a stretch of riverbank in the west. From the Kreuzberg side, the West Berliners playing badminton and walking their dogs can discern the expressions on the faces of the East Berlin housewives hanging up their washing. But they do not salute each other, or even risk a sly wave. They stare at each other like hostile cats living in the same house. As the Berlin writer Peter Schneider says, 'for Germans in the west, the wall became a mirror that told them day after day who was the fairest of them all. Whether there was life beyond the death strip soon mattered only to pigeons and cats.'

Immense numbers of people have been added and subtracted from the city, which absorbed them gratefully like a sponge. The city of Berlin was always something of a parvenu amongst the grown-up capitals of renaissance Europe. It shared the curiously unformed, shapeless character of Prussia, expanding and contracting east and then west like a piece of ectoplasm, forever in search of an identity. French Huguenots in the eighteenth century were followed by Jews in the nineteenth. In the twentieth century, in the nightmare years of war, occupation and partition, when there was a brisk trade in human flesh among the starving citizenry, several million refugees were poured into the swollen corpse from Prussia, Silesia, the Sudetenland and the Baltic. And although East Berlin is not as cosmopolitan as its western half, there continues a steady trickle of immigrants from the less favoured towns of Brandenburg, Saxony and Thuringia, who blithely ignore the web of laws against taking up residence in Berlin without a permit. 'Find a true Berliner and he belongs in a museum,' is a remark one often hears. And no wonder, for as rural East Germans often grumble, 'everything goes to Berlin'.

The city is a stage where cast and sets have altered with bewildering speed. The small seat of minor princelings became the enlightened capital of Frederican Prussia which vanished into the glittering cankered rose of Bismarck's phoney empire. Then came the decadent playground of the 1920s, tumbling into the throne of Hitler's Reich before emerging as the capital of the DDR – the 'first socialist state on German soil'. Fortune has whirled fast and has left everyone looking exhausted with the costume changes.

Each of Berlin's changing faces has left its mark on the next. Berlin is a Prussian city. It is bossy and authoritarian in public, indulgent and a little camp in private. The Berliners took their socialism seriously and remained loyal to the Social Democrats right up until Hitler's seizure of power in 1933. East Germany is perhaps the only country in eastern Europe where a good many people have not given up trying to make classical Marxism work. The Prussian state was tolerant of its citizens' religious and moral foibles when they did not contradict the interests of the state. Today East Germany is the only country in the eastern bloc where the open profession of homosexuality is no bar to a career, even in the Communist party.

There were six churches in medieval Berlin and Kölln. The parish churches of St Nicholas and St Mary still remain. There were also a Franciscan monastery and the church of the Holy Hospital by Spandauer Tor. In Kölln were the parish churches of St Peter and a Dominican monastery. The church of St Nicholas in the Nichlas quarter was begun in 1232. It is the oldest church in Berlin, though it now functions as a museum of the March of Brandenburg. Inside is the Spandau Madonna of 1290 and a collection of fifteenth-century liturgical vessels. In the visitors' book I read the last inscription: 'What a stupid idea, turning a church into a museum.'

There was a time when the Old Berlin of the Brandenburg March was an embarrassment to the leaders of the DDR. Walther Ulbricht, who dominated public life for the first quarter of a century, saw his little portion of Prussia on the banks of the Spree as a mere stepping stone to the formation of an all-German socialist state. Then the DDR cultivated an 'all-German' mentality which stressed its historical descent from the German peasant rebels of the sixteenth century and the revolutionaries of the nineteenth. As if to distance themselves from the Hohenzollern past, the bombed remains of the royal palace in the Berlin Schloss were swept away and the centre of Berlin was rebuilt with tall tower blocks. Much of Berlin still reflects the Ulbricht era. His spirit hovers over the 'Allees', the grey and windswept boulevards that stretch out of the city centre towards the suburbs.

The DDR has changed. A whole generation grew up who had seen nothing of the German lands to the west of the old borders of the March of Brandenburg. The success of the 'economic miracle' in West Germany shattered Ulbricht's dream of a united Germany under the domination of the Communist party. With his departure, the DDR found a new *raison d'être* in the cultivation of what they call 'a separate DDR mentality'. But change of emphasis required a new attitude to history so as to prove that the establishment of a separate German state in the lands of the old March of Brandenburg was more than the result of an unsavoury bargain between the great powers.

And so the old ghosts of Prussian history returned. Frederick the Great reappeared on his horse in the Unter den Linden. The *burgermeisters'* houses on the banks of the Spree were restored to their old finery. Around the St Nicholas church an entire medieval quarter was rebuilt with pitched roofs and old pubs. Around the St Sophie church, the old shops were reconstructed with wooden, swinging signs. The anonymous and spartan cafés of the 1950s and 1960s gave way to intimate pubs, or *kneipen*, with diamond-paned windows, walls lined with shields depicting the arms of Berlin, and floors of black and white tiles, as if from a Vermeer painting.

Nothing remains of the old baroque frontage of the Alexanderplatz, which was cleared away after the war to make way for the gleaming glass panels of the East German parliament, the *Volkskammer*. The square has now expanded to include another of the medieval churches of Berlin, St Mary's, Berlin's oldest functioning place of worship. The church dates from 1270, was largely rebuilt in 1380, and contains an unusual fresco of the Dance of Death, which dates from the period after the great plague visited the city in the 1480s. The vestry houses one of those faintly subversive bookshops where they sell 'alternative' postcards.

The Thirty Years' War took its toll on Berlin and reduced the number of inhabitants by one third. In 1648 there were no more than 6,000 people in Berlin and Kölln, inhabiting a mere 750 dwellings. But the end of the Thirty Years' War proved to be an era of new beginnings in the city. In the last quarter of the seventeenth century the 'Great Prince', as the DDR now refers to Prince Frederick William, established several new suburbs. A seal of the year 1700 shows a small princely *residenzstadt* in which the original core of Berlin and Kölln had now expanded into the new districts of Friedrichswerder, Friedrichstadt and Dorotheenstadt, the last named after the 'Great Prince's' wife.

Berlin was changing from a minor princely residence into a European capital. In 1696 the Academy of Arts was founded, bringing the architects Andreas Schluter and Johann Arnold Nehring to Berlin. In 1701, Frederick I was crowned the first King of Prussia and his insistence that the seat of the Hohenzollerns should rival the other princely courts of Europe led to a new intensive programme of building. In the 1730s the Crown Prince and Crown Princess's palaces were built and these were soon followed by the construction of a great boulevard, the Unter den Linden.

The arrival of the French protestant refugees in the 1680s altered the demographic character of the city. Berlin became less insular and more secular. The first great influx of immigrants from France occurred after the revocation of the Edict of Nantes in 1685. Their piety and prosperity is commemorated by the small eighteenth-century jewel of the 'French church' in the Platz der Academie.

The square is one of the finest classical views in Europe. On either side are the twin and classical monuments of the German Dom and the French Dom, facing each other across the square like sisters. In the middle is the Opera. And tucked beside the French Dom is the French church. It is now used by the Lutheran church, but its name perpetuates the memory of the French protestants who were welcomed into Berlin by the Great Prince.

The million-strong Huguenot community in France were, like the Quakers in England, an industrious and unpopular minority. Under the Edict of Nantes France avoided civil war by granting the French protestants certain privileges. The Huguenots had no place at the court of the Sun King Louis XIV, however, and in 1685 the Edict of Nantes was revoked and the great majority of protestants were expelled, or fled, from France for ever.

Two hundred thousand Huguenots fled to Brandenburg, Hesse, Switzerland and England. James II of England was dismayed by the prospect of thousands of committed Calvinists settling in his domains. To Frederick William, however, the arrival of such a multifariously talented people was a boon. On 29 October 1685 Frederick answered the Revocation of the Edict of Nantes with the Edict of Potsdam. The Edict offered free exercise of their religion to any French protestants wishing to settle in Brandenburg-Prussia. Some 20,000 Huguenots took up the Great Prince's offer, of whom about 5,000 settled in Berlin. A further Edict gave the French refugees the status of Prussian citizens. In the small residence this influx made a great impact. Around the turn of the eighteenth century it was said that one third of the city's inhabitants were of French stock.

At first they held their services in the local Lutheran churches. But with royal consent, a French church was erected in Friedrichstadt in 1705, in what is today the Platz der Academie. This church then lent its name to the neighbouring 'French' Dom that was erected beside it some eighty years later.

The fate of catholics in Berlin was rather different. Berlin's second cathedral, St Hedwig's, is the seat of the catholic archdiocese of Berlin. It is as restrained in its classicism as the Dom is exuberant in mock-baroque, as if the building's very discretion reflected the uncertain relationship between catholics and the state of Prussia.

The reformation did not arrive in Berlin until the late 1530s, which was relatively late by German standards. Prince Joachim was unwilling to commit himself thoroughly to either camp. Under his successors, however, Brandenburg-Prussia adhered thoroughly to the Lutheran cause. Permission for catholics to hear Mass was not granted until the time of the Great Prince, in 1680. Even then the catholics of Berlin had to wait until 1722 for a church of their own, when a chapel was built between Leipziger and Klausener strasse. In 1746, however, they received a royal patent from Potsdam to erect the church of St Hedwig, which was completed in 1755 in the style of the Pantheon in Paris.

Bismarck waged war against the growing influence of the catholic church after the unification of Germany under Prussian auspices in 1871. The new empire included the catholic rural states of the south, but the catholic church in Prussia, like that in contemporary England, was largely a church of the poorer classes and immigrants.

St Hedwig's did not become a cathedral until the 1930s. Unlike the evangelical church, which reluctantly acceded to official pressure to cultivate a 'separate DDR mentality' by separating itself from the church in West Germany, the catholic church in East Germany remains oblivious to Berlin's post-war division. The catholic bishop of Berlin remains pastor of both sides of the city.

The absolutism of the Hohenzollerns led to Berlin taking on a different complexion from London or Amsterdam. Berlin became the capital, not of a state which possessed an army, but as Mirabeau's witticism suggested, 'an army which possessed a state'. In spite of civic opposition, Berlin became a garrison town by 1657 and by the end of the eighteenth century a fifth of the population were soldiers.

The Hohenzollern prince Frederick II robbed Berlin of its civic independence in the mid-fifteenth century. The Berlin town hall

9

remained a humble red-brick structure. The huge red-brick town hall which now stands beside Spandauestrasse dates from the 1860s. Instead of a town hall or parliament, the Hohenzollerns erected a royal castle, known as the Berlin Schloss. Nothing now remains of the 'dark and dreadful prison' which filled Princess Victoria with so much dread when she arrived from Britain in 1858 as the bride of Prince Frederick William of Prussia.

Although the royal castle has disappeared, the adjacent royal cathedral, the Berliner Dom, remains in uncomfortable juxtaposition to the East German parliament, the *Volkskammer*. The fifteenth-century Berlin Schloss contained a chapel, which was dedicated by a papal bull to St Erasmus. In 1536, Prince Joachim, who rebuilt the Schloss in renaissance style, donated the chapel to the Dominicans. The monks used it for only two years, for in 1538 the church became protestant. From 1545 the church became the burial place of the Prussian royal family. It was rebuilt in a manner more suitable to its ceremonial and royal functions in the 1740s and again during the brief reign of Emperor Frederick William II. The rebuilding of the cathedral was one of the few projects of this liberal prince that were continued with any enthusiasm by his bumptious successor, Emperor William II.

BERLIN

Revolutionaries

'The revolution is splendid. Everything else is rubbish.'
Rosa Luxemburg

ROSA LUXEMBURG square, Clara Zetkin street, Karl Liebknecht street. The streetscape of Berlin is a great memorial to the knights and queens and some of the pawns who strode across the chessboard of the Social Democratic Party of Germany which at the turn of the century was the largest political organisation in the world professing the revolutionary ideals of Karl Marx and Friedrich Engels.

Rosa Luxemburg was by origin a Polish Jewess. Flamboyant, brilliantly incisive, lovable and almost infinitely capable of bestowing love on others, hers was the most exhilarating revolutionary spirit to have come out of Poland since Adam Mickiewicz. She was indifferent on the subject of Polish independence, however, which may explain why she has received no public memorial in her native land other than a light-bulb factory.

In Berlin she has an entire square to herself. In the East German pantheon of revolutionary deities, this places her below Karl Liebknecht, who has a four-lane highway, but above Clara Zetkin, who has only a small avenue.

Whilst crossing the square, I thought of that feisty lady, 'small and looking neat in her summer dress, with such magnetism in her eyes'. Rosa Luxemburg was emphatically committed to the revolutionary left wing of German politics. Her socialist convictions, however, were shot through with an intense humanity which seems to have been lost in the composition of the German Democratic Republic, in spite of the cracked smile it officially wears nowadays.

One wonders whether those who named the square after Rosa Luxemburg were aware of her much remembered maxim that 'freedom is always for the one who thinks differently', or of her abiding distrust of Lenin. Irrespective of the rights and wrongs of her political opinions, any free spirit must admire her 'damnable longing for happiness' and her determination to 'haggle for my daily portion with the stubbornness of a mule'.

In 1918 she stood both at the height of her influence and at the edge of the precipice that would lead to her death. Berlin was in a state of ferment. The war was lost. The Emperor William II was babbling incoherently from his military headquarters in Spa. The mobs were out in Berlin and among them roamed the bands of disillusioned and demobilised soldiers known as the Freikorps, who were eager for the blood of those they imagined had 'stabbed Germany in the back'.

The moderates among the Social Democrats declared a republic. In the subsequent dizziness, the left wing of the Social Democrats, known as the 'Spartacists', led by Rosa Luxemburg and Karl Liebknecht, attempted a coup against the Social Democratic leaders, who were already hand in glove with the old generals and 'cabbage junkers' of Prussia. Lenin went wild with joy that the 'German Sparatcusbund with its world famous leaders' was attacking the 'robber bourgeoisie'. His hopes seemed justified when the new minister of defence had to flee from the centre of Berlin and take refuge in a girls' school in the suburb of Dahlem.

A revolution could not succeed, however, when those attacking the Chancellery proved reluctant to tread on the newly cut grass, still less when one of the divisions who had been sent by Karl Liebknecht to occupy the ministry of war agreed to go away when it was pointed out by the defenders that the besiegers' orders had not been correctly countersigned.

Rosa moved from one address to another, as if aware that the threads of fate were shortly to tie her down at last. 'I have been expelled from all the hotels in Potsdam Square,' she told her colleague Clara Zetkin. In the end she was clubbed to death by a soldier called Vogel, who was subsequently awarded a pension by Hitler. The leadership of revolutionary Germany passed to less imaginative spirits like Clara Zetkin, who were to become Stalinist drones.

In the Unter den Linden there is a museum of German revolutionary history. Inside the exhibition is a photograph taken in 1945 of a ser-ious-looking but rather dashing young man, with squeaky clean fea-tures and a shock of blond hair. It could be the portrait of an ambitious curate, though of evangelical rather than anglo-catholic persuasion. It is, in fact, Erich Honecker, the current leader of East Germany.

At the time in which the photograph was taken, Mr Honecker was the leader of the Free German Youth and a relatively minor star in the constellation which orbited Walter Ulbricht, the dominant force in East German politics for the first quarter of a century follow-ing the Second World War. Mr Ulbricht was not the leader of the East German Communists after the war. That honour belonged to Wilhelm Pieck, a genial old man who was kicked upstairs before very long to become the first president of the new German Democratic Republic. But Mr Ulbricht was both the power behind and, before very long, the power sitting on the throne. Douglas Botting's *In the Ruins of the Reich* preserves a vignette of how Mr Ulbricht knocked the East German Communists into shape and knocked out the spirit of Rosa Luxemburg at the same time.

There was a meeting soon after the end of the Second World War of some Communists in Berlin in order to discuss the question of abortions for German women who had been raped by Russian soldiers. Mr Ulbricht terminated the discussion as follows:

'There can be no question of it. I regard the discussion as closed.'

There were cries of opposition from the floor who were hitherto accustomed to the notion of free debate.

'We can't do it. We must discuss it,' shouted one. Ulbricht faced the meeting with an angry frown.

'I repeat,' he said sharply, 'I regard the discussion on this subject as closed. I will not allow the debate to be continued.'

In the years that followed, Mr Ulbricht 'would not allow the debate to be continued' on many other matters either.

The Bertholt Brecht house in Chaussee street is a small, comfortably furnished apartment. It is decorated with many mementoes of the playwright's last years in Berlin after the years of exile from Hitler's Germany, in America and Denmark among other places. In the kitchen is a fine set of blue porcelain crockery. The apartment is a reminder that some German intellectuals preferred life in Ulbricht's domain on the Oder-Neisse to that of Adenauer on the Rhine. In this little flat overlooking the graves of Hegel and Fichter lived Brecht and his last wife Helene Weigel, who became the director of the Berliner Ensemble, a theatre devoted to perpetuating her husband's works.

Some have seen Brecht's deliberate choice to live in the east rather than the west of Berlin as an example of the perfidy of intellectuals, who opposed Hitler only subsequently to genuflect before Stalin. Perhaps what is most surprising is that an artist who had spent so much time in western Europe and America was ever made welcome in East Germany at all. For after the irreparable division of Germany in 1949, the so-called 'German road to Socialism' which had been advocated by the Communists up till then was promptly abandoned for a rapid forced march to Moscow which threw all those who had wintered in the west rather than in Moscow under some suspicion.

The East German road to socialism has never been as clear-cut as in the rest of eastern Europe, however. For in East Germany the Communists gained power not through a decisive *putsch* but almost through osmosis. The democratic organs of government set up throughout Germany in 1945 were never torn up at the roots; they merely ossified. In East Germany today there remain large Liberal and Christian Democratic parties, though they lead a somewhat *piano* existence. The public face of the Christian Democrats, for example, is maintained largely through the management of decorous and vaguely churchy bookshops. The front pages of their newspapers are no different from those of the Communist papers. It is only in the back pages, among the art columns and features, that one notices the difference. What the Communists will not tolerate is another party of the left. There are no Social Democrats; a shot-gun marriage with the Communists in 1946 brought them into the new 'Socialist Unity Party'.

Among these latter was Bertholt Brecht's friend and admirer, Otto

Grotewohl. Mr Grotewohl was the classic Vicar of Bray. A long-time Social Democrat, he became Prime Minister of East Germany in 1949, principally on account of the services he had rendered towards the unification of Communists and Social Democrats three years previously. This position he determined on never losing. He followed every twist and turn of the Byzantine Stalinist politics of the 1950s. He became deft in the language of the Cold War and was able to include the phrase 'proletarian vanguard' several times in a single sentence. He remained loyal to his artistic friends, however, and Brecht was among them.

What has become of the party of Rosa Luxemburg and Walther Ulbricht. Of the dazzling little figure in a white summer dress, pleading from a soap box? Of the man with a goatee beard bellowing to an audience of terrified Communists in a Berlin hall lit by a single light bulb? What has become of the thrilling days of the Cold War and the erection of the 'anti-fascist wall'?

I arrived in Berlin to find the Socialist Unity Party paper *Neues Deutschland* running a series of breathless articles commemorating the day in 1961 when the wall was built. The Christian Democratic papers passed over the event, not because their editors were any the less under the thumb of the ruling party, but presumably from some sensitivity to what the readership could stomach.

There was also a supplementary pull-out. Mug-shots of East German border guards who had apparently been shot by the imperialists on the other side during the course of duty. I was mesmerised for some time over my mid-morning *Kaffee und Kuchen* by their dopy and trusting faces.

I met only two members of the ruling Socialist Unity Party in Berlin, a gangling young man called Constantin and his boyfriend, Werner. I met Constantin late at night in an old pub in Alte Schoenhauser street. I remember it well, because the air was full of smoke, the Pet Shop Boys were singing 'Heart Beat' and I was sitting opposite two women who were horribly drunk. One was crying. Shortly after I arrived she stood up, tottered a few steps into the street and vomited noisily and audibly into the gutter. It was then that Constantin interrupted my furious scribbling in my notebook with the unsolicited news that: 'Horst Wessel died here, you know. You know the "Horst Wessel song" I suppose?'

I gamely tried to hum a few stanzas of this old Nazi ballad.

'He didn't die for political reasons, you know,' the stranger continued with a knowing wink, which was entirely lost on me.

I had no idea how Horst Wessel died, but said: 'He didn't? Really?'

Constantin gave me a cryptic smile. 'This was *notorious* area before the war and after as well. Pimps, whores . . . that sort of thing.'

We sat till two in the morning in the bar, thereby disproving the notion that everything shuts in East Berlin by midnight. I emerged with an invitation to dine at Constantin's flat the following evening near the Frankurter gate.

In between picking the dandruff out of each other's hair and fiddling with each other's dungarees, Constantin and Werner resembled all the other ambitious but incurious yuppies I have met. By their own account they spent most of their time dining out in private restaurants, rummaging on bric-à-brac stalls for antiques for their flat, spying on their neighbours (they didn't quite phrase it that way) and going on holiday in Rostock.

Neither Constantin nor Werner was remotely interested in travelling to or knowing about life in the west. Nor was there much mileage to be got out of raising the subjects of Mr Dubcek's 'socialism with a human face', Mr Gorbachev's reforms, or the Berlin Wall. Only one aspect of life in Great Britain had caught their imagination: the putting up of pink plaques in London to commemorate various gay 'alumni'. They both hoped the Berlin district of the Socialist Unity Party would follow suit by erecting similar pink triangles to commemorate German homosexuals who had been murdered by the Nazis.

I felt that Constantin and Werner had both missed their true vocations on one of the innumerable sub-committees of the late Greater London Council. Even when that institution was at the height of its powers, however, I doubt that it had the largesse to reward its lieutenants so fulsomely as does the Berlin district of the Socialist Unity Party. Werner and Constantin occupied the larger and most comfortably furnished apartment I set eyes upon in East Germany.

BERLIN

Prenzlauerberg

I went to a basement tavern near the Schlesicher
bahnhof where you paid a Mark and saw an
extraordinary cabaret programme of sexual freaks,
harumphrodites and the like. Young male prostitutes
walked the streets. A dozen, a score of resorts where
homosexuals of both sexes could meet plied a thriving
trade, the young men dressed as girls, the girls trying
to look like men.

Douglas Reed, Insanity Fair

'WHAT ON EARTH is a harumphrodite?' I thought as I wondered
into the Schonhauser Ecke. 'Will I find one here?'

The Ecke is the naughtiest café in eastern Europe and a tribute
to Berlin's continuing indulgence towards the more flamboyant members of society. In England such an establishment would be secreted
away in some obscure alleyway behind a disguised door to conceal
it from the hostile and enquiring eyes of the public. But the Ecke
is on the junction of the two main thoroughfares that sweep out
of the city centre through the suburbs of Prenzlauerberg and only
a large glass window divides the antics within from the view of the
weary housewives pushing their shopping trolleys up the Prenzlauer
Allee towards Pankow suburb.

Prenzlauerberg is not an ordinary suburb of East Berlin. It is
'the Greenwich village of the DDR', as one West Berliner ruefully

described it. The high-ceilinged nineteenth-century apartments which look out over spacious squares suggest that in its heyday the area was highly desirable, much like Kensington in London. With the rapid expansion of the city in the 1880s, the middle classes emigrated from the city centre to the greener suburbs of Weissensee and Pankow, which were further out of the city centre, Prenzlauerberg assumed the more working-class character which it possessed before the Second World War.

There were a multitude of small shops, tailors, shoemakers, book-shops, tobacconists whose trade signs are still visible over the door-ways underneath the carelessly applied whitewash. On the bare walls are the faded advertisements for pre-war companies and the sight of these mementoes of the old Germany gives the streets an eerie feeling.

These small businesses continued to ply their trade long after the end of the war and the division of Berlin into separate and hostile zones, and only disappeared during the socialisation of small busi-nesses in the 1950s and early 1960s. The flight of this entrepreneurial class in 1960 and 1961 was one of the principal reasons behind the sudden decision to erect the Wall.

One or two streets in Prenzlauerberg, like the splendid Husemann-strasse, have been immaculately restored to turn of the century style with an almost intimidating eye for historic exactitude. The street has been painted and re-cobbled; 'original' nineteenth-century adver-tisements have been painted artfully on to the walls; the shops have been installed with *fin-de-siècle* shop windows; the street signs have been replaced with signs suspended from old gas lamp-posts and engraved in Gothic letters. Even the post office has been gutted and turned into a kind of museum. It is a wonder that the people serving the stamps haven't been ordered to dress up in nineteenth-century clothes as well, for when the East Germans restore, they restore with a vengeance, as there are no private or commercial objections which have to be taken into consideration.

As no one else in East Berlin cares two hoots about the appearance of their state-owned apartments, stumbling upon Husemannstrasse is a startling experience, as the surrounding avenues have mostly crumbled into a state of such disrepair that the moulded cornices have come to resemble a natural rockface. During the last decade,

however, these dingy but romantic apartment blocks in Prenzlauerberg have become the favourite residence of 'alternative' East
Germans and intellectuals.

In a society as ordered and conformist as the DDR, the 'alternative'
East Germans are immediately recognisable from the mainline DDR
citizens around them. These mainliners are equally easy to spot. You
see them in small family outings on trains, big Hans and little Hans
in matching green *lederhosen*, whilst mama in blonde braids looks
satisfied and fecund. Mainline DDR citizens queue outside historic
castles and museums for hours with such forced joviality you would
think they positively enjoyed the wait, whilst the 'alternative' Germans and misfits like myself smoke cigarettes and whine and curse
at the delays.

In middle age the mainline DDR folk become still more pronoun-
cedly bourgeois. You see them walking down the Unter den Linden,
one man and his bosomy wife, arm in arm and wearing an expression
of quiet delight that a land as wonderful as the DDR really does
exist. On Sundays they take their wives out to the posher new restaurants in the city and they deliberately sit at your table if you are on
your own to show you what good *genossen*, comrades, they are. Before
they sit down, they both address you with a warm 'Guten Taaag',
and finish off with an equally warm 'Auf Weidersehen' when they
leave.

'Alternative' East German society is by no means politically hostile
to the order of things in the DDR. It comprises a rainbow coalition
of polo-necked artists, underground poets, ecology freaks, long-
haired students, jazz addicts, camp homosexuals, radical Christians,
and people who just want to dress a little outrageously. Many of
them hang around churches, which have a reputation in Berlin as
havens of political and sexual tolerance. In most east European countries this 'alternative' society is too small a minority to form a collective identity, but in Berlin they have an entire quarter to themselves
in Prenzlauerberg. Pretty much anything goes in the Prenzlauerberg
bars – many of which stay open until the small hours – whether
it is picking up girls, or boys, passing around illegal publications,
or just getting wildly drunk. The police make no move against Prenzlauerberg's seamy side, as they prefer this cultural rather than political
dissent to exist in the open where they can keep an eye on things.

I once asked why the police never appeared in one of Prenzlauerberg's crazier late-late bars and was told, 'The police probably *are* here. You just can't recognise them.'

Even the churches in Prenzlauerberg have an 'alternative' flavour. I met one family who had driven all the way from Dresden to visit the ecology bookshop that is housed in the hall of the Zion church. Over the doorway hung the following revealing notice:

> Diocese of Berlin Brandenburg. Professor Stephen Lanzendorff (Leipzig) will deliver a lecture on the subject of 'Safe Sex'. Title: 'Sex and Fun.' There will be tea and a discussion with the pastor afterwards. You are all heartily welcome.

The family from Dresden read this notice with as much interest as I did and noted all the relevant details.

In the Schonhauser Ecke there were a number of tables artfully scattered around a large parquet floor. Upon each table stood a small Egyptian-style obelisk from which protruded a single rose.

'Monika, darling,' came a melodic voice from the other side of the room, addressing the waitress. The voice belonged to a plump young man sitting with six of his mates.

'Six cream torten, Monika,' the voice continued. 'No, I said *six* cakes, not *sex* . . . oh isn't she perfectly *awful*?'

I sat next to a soldier called Mike. He wasn't actually a soldier. He just dressed like one in green battle fatigues and later confessed that he was really a mental nurse from Halle.

Mike made a very imposing picture, the body of a Prussian officer having been successfully grafted on to the mannerisms of an English 'queen'. A pair of incredibly long legs encased in thigh-high boots, of the kind favoured by the Kaiser during the First World War, tapered off in the distance under the table.

He was bold and confident as only a Berlin queen could be, and he stared at me with a predatory grin as I grew more and more nervous, waiting for Monika's attention. By the time Monika arrived I was so tongue-tied that I messed up my order and got it back to front.

'I *think* he is after a fruit cream cake and a cup of coffee, Monika,' Mike laconically informed the waitress, with his patronising grin widening even further. This put me into a tremendous sulk, upon

which he immediately changed tack and began talking in that animated, forceful Berlin manner, about his hobbies and his work permit
and his holiday in Poland, as if life and death depended on our having
this conversation.

Mike was a regular Prussian, dizzy and serious by turns, as he
weaved deftly between low-life anecdotes which illustrated his sexual
prowess with the lads (a few girls were thrown in as well to spice
things up) and remarks like, 'Everyone should read the Bible and
Das Kapital. They are the two most important books in the world.'

Mike took me to a club in the Buschallee, which he said was a
night extension of the Schonhauser Ecke. It was not a very imposing
discotheque and would not have rated high marks in London or New
York, or for that matter West Berlin, but Mike said it was the best
they had.

'Is it the only "alternative" disco in Berlin?' I asked Mike.

'It's the only one in the entire DDR,' he answered knowledgeably.

A large crowd of people were waiting outside the door. They
formed themselves into a kind of scrum, beating on the door with
their fists and shouting for the doorman's attention. From the other
side of the door could be heard the doorman's muffled cries of rage
as he pushed on the other side to stop the crowd from breaking
in.

'The DDR could certainly do with a few more clubs,' said Mike
wearily, before striding into the *mêlée*. 'Hang on to my arm,' he suggested. 'If you get lost, wave a five-pound note. I promise you that
the crowd will part like the waters of the Red Sea.'

The door was finally flung open, but barring the way to this army
of Teutonic Knights was not a doorman but a six-foot blonde woman
dressed in an azure leotard. She quickly scanned the crowd, dismissing
with a brief wave of the hand those who didn't make the grade,
and picking out a lucky few who were young, beautiful . . . and Mike.

'I used to know her when she was a man, before she had the operation,' Mike whispered confidentially as we squeezed past this huge
amazon and into the club. As a gruff old *hausfrau* took our coats
and bags, I wanted to ask Mike about this 'operation'. Had it been
done, as it were, on the National Health in the DDR? How long
did one have to wait? How many others had had the same operation?
I searched for Mike but he had disappeared into the crowd.

Mike spent most of the evening gyrating on the dance floor with an immensely overweight woman in her forties, breaking off to do a tango with the transvestite in the blue leotard. As both of them were well over six feet tall it made a superb sight. It was past one o'clock in the morning when I told Mike I had decided to return to my palatial hotel off the Unter den Linden. 'Excuse me one minute,' said Mike, 'I have to make sleeping arrangements.' He strode over the dance floor in his seven-league boots to a little fellow who had been eyeing him all evening with a mixture of hope and despair. In his livid green tie and stiff white collar he reminded me of a gecko, but upon this diminutive courtier the kindly eye of the Prussian officer had rested.

Looking extraordinarily inappropriate but somehow perfect in his mock-officer's uniform, he inclined his head to whisper in the little fellow's ear. There was, as expected, an eager nod and a dazzling smile from the smaller party, which Mike barely acknowledged as he strode back to escort me to my hotel.

The tram skidded and hissed its way through the streets of Prenz-lauerberg, the light from the windows illuminating in brief flashes, like snapshots from a camera, a sequence of punks and empty door-ways. The tram screeched its way round a corner from the narrow avenues of Prenzlauerberg into an empty neon-lit boulevard in the centre of the city. I alighted near the Alexanderplatz with its illumi-nated needle-shaped radio tower puncturing the heavens. Mike waved goodbye from the doorway of the tram, a large black silhouette against the bright light of the carriage. 'Don't forget to send me a visa,' he shouted as the doors slammed shut and the tram shuddered on its way.

BERLIN

The rabbi

> *Goering:* How many synagogues were burnt?
> *Heydrich:* Altogether one hundred and one synagogues
> were destroyed in the Third Reich by fire, seventy-six
> were demolished and seven thousand five hundred
> shops were destroyed.
> *Goering:* What do you mean by 'destroyed by fire?'
> *Heydrich:* They were partly burnt down and partly burnt
> out.
>
> From the minutes taken after kristallnacht *on 12 November 1938*

'WELL DID I, or did I *not* give the Lutherans *hell*?' inquired the rabbi with a chuckle that suggested he already knew the answer, as we drove away from the St Stephen's Institute in the suburb of Wahnsee.

'You certainly did.' (He really did. There was a row of nuns who applauded his speech by banging their knuckles hard on the desks where they were sitting.)

'Well I do not mind other people lecturing Israel about the West Bank, but I am *not* going to be lectured about Israel by *Germans*. These Lutherans need a rabbi all to themselves. They are so insensitive and anti-semitic. You only have to read what Luther said about the Jews to understand why.'

We sped down the Friedrichstrasse towards the rabbi's flat. I wondered what had happened to the speed limit. Was this some kind of DDR atonement for the errors of the past, that their one and only rabbi was exempted from all speed restrictions? It was the kind of thing they *would* do.

'I see you have a chauffeur.'

The rabbi nodded. 'Uh huh. The DDR have kept their side of the bargain. They look after me. They have provided me with a flat. Mind you, the chauffeur probably works for someone else as well.' He winked. The chauffeur kept his eye on the road.

The rabbi's flat had a spartan, uninhabited air. As he bustled into the small adjoining kitchen to make the tea, I scanned some of the correspondence that was strewn on the table. Amongst it was a telegram from President Reagan congratulating the rabbi on twenty-five years in the ministry.

'Yes, you *may* read my mail.'

I jumped in my chair. The rabbi had surprised me by returning so silently. 'You obviously have connections in high places.'

'I have two sons *working* in the White House. Good jobs and highly paid. Not bad for an immigrant's son, eh?'

He poured me a cup of tea. 'They didn't think too highly of my coming to the DDR, that's for sure.'

It seemed an obvious question. What was an American rabbi doing in the DDR? He paused. It was a question which he had obviously asked himself a lot without ever providing himself with a satisfactory answer.

'There are times when I would gladly answer that question. There are other times when I would not, and this is one of them.'

We drank the tea in silence. I looked out of the window. The streets of East Berlin always look curiously bare. With my back to him, the rabbi began to talk, as if to himself.

'There was a job to be done here. Something needed to be revived. There has been no rabbi here for over twenty years.'

East Germany's Jewish population is numerically insignificant, numbering at the outset about 2,000, of whom only a few hundred are registered as members of Jewish organisations. They possess one active synagogue in Rykestrasse. The rabbi told me that shortly after the war a handful of remarkable individuals, including one English Communist Jewess, returned to their homes in East Berlin in an immensely brave symbolic gesture. But most of the Jewish community who remained in the DDR were those who were too old or too indifferent to their religious heritage to be of service in building up a new generation of East German Jews. By the 1980s the older generation were dying away and many of the young had emigrated. Their survival, however, is a matter of great importance to the government of the DDR, which is why they were prepared to go to America to find a rabbi who was willing to come to minister to East Germany's ageing and endangered Jewish community.

When I turned round the rabbi's face was discouraged, which was not surprising considering the mammoth task he had set himself.

'There are more funerals than weddings,' he said. 'We have been waiting months for repairs to be done to the synagogue in Ryke-strasse. I try to be assertive but some of the congregation have forgotten how to do anything but cringe. I sometimes feel like a doctor whose only function is to make the patients more comfortable so that he can die easy.'

I was shown out by the rabbi's chauffeur. As I went out of the door I suddenly imagined he was going to arrest me. The rabbi's last advice had been to go to the Senefelderplatz cemetery. 'You'll see what I mean about anti-semitism in the DDR.' I walked to the cemetery past the blackened and burnt-out oriental façade of the Oranienburger strasse synagogue. On the outside wall of this vast cathedral-sized building, where the rich and powerful had once given thanks for their happy estate in Bismarck's Prussia, hung a notice which read: 'Never forget.'

Officially the East Germans have certainly not forgotten. The West Germans paid millions of deutschmarks in compensation and the East Germans did not. The reasons for this were both practical and ideological. The Nazis executed the Communists and left-wing Social Democrats with as much efficiency as they executed Jews. When this coalition seized power in the eastern zone of Germany between 1946 and 1947, they did so as the heirs of the dedicated anti-Nazi resistance and had no intention of acknowledging their succession to Hitler by paying his bills. But behind the ideological bravado of refusing to pay was the fact that they couldn't pay, for whilst the Americans were building up the new Federal Republic as a barrier against the spread of Communism, the Russians were busily stripping the eastern zone of everything of conceivable value for reparations, even down to the typewriters.

Instead the East Germans have attempted to educate the coming generations in the tragedy that befell the German Jews, in the belief that prevention is better than cure. Part of the training for joining the Free German Youth, the DDR's near-compulsory youth organisation, involves visiting concentration camps within the borders of the DDR, such as Dachau. The written material provided for these occasions gives a place to the apparently heroic resistance of the German communists that is almost equal to that given to the vastly superior numbers of Jews who perished in the camps, but there is undoubtedly a serious intention behind the signs that say: 'Never forget.'

A high level of public awareness was suggested by the fact that there was scarcely a town that I visited in the DDR in which one of the churches did not have some exhibition about the life and contribution of the Jews to the various cities in which they lived. In the 'peace museum' of the church of St Mary's in Berlin, for example, there were many photographs depicting the synagogues of Berlin and the lives of Jewish immigrants.

These exhibitions were usually accompanied by a lament about the failure of the evangelical church to resist the work of the Nazi 'Reichsbishop' whom Hitler installed to 'purify' the life of the church from Jewish elements.

The exhibitions did not take a 'class attitude' by representing only the sufferings of the exploited working-class Jews. The best of its kind was an exhibition in Erfurt detailing the life of a single family from their arrival in the city in the seventeenth century until their extermination in the 1940s. It began with scratched and torn documents testifying to the family's arrival in the city, moving through the centuries until the age of the camera, when the family came to life before our eyes in faded sepia photographs which depicted them in the full but fatal bloom of Bismarckian prosperity, the men stiff and proud in their wing collars, the women plump and crinolined. The photographs ended in the 1930s, by which time the young ladies in their bustle dresses had become ancient and smiling great-grandmothers, clutching fat babies in their gnarled fingers.

The last panel was simply a roll call of the different camps in which these ancient and smiling great-grandmothers and bouncing babies from Erfurt had perished.

Some East Germans have forgotten in spite of it all. I followed the rabbi's advice and visited the Senefelderplatz cemetery, where I found that a sizeable number of the tombstones had been recently upturned and even smashed into pieces. None of the perpetrators of this crime had been caught. The tomb of Benjamin Schlesinger and his brother Nathan was still there, however, a hefty tomb, as most German tombs are. Inscribed below the dates was a disturbing epitaph:

> Better a good name than costly oil.
> Better the day of one's death
> Than the day of one's birth.

BERLIN

Saturday afternoon in Potsdam

THAT 'DREADFUL Prussian pride' which so grieved Queen Victoria's beloved Albert emanated above all from the Berlin suburb of Potsdam, where his hapless daughter, Princess Victoria of Prussia, spent much of her time in the Neue Palais being watched by Bismarck's spies.

Potsdam lies in relation to Berlin as does Hampton Court to London, but as it lies on the western side of Allied Berlin, it now takes a good two hours to reach the town from East Berlin by a complicated system of trains and buses.

This exhausting journey did not, unfortunately, deter a vast crowd of Berliners from making the trip on the same day that I did. Tired, angry, some even in tears, they arrived in a heaving throng at the railway station and flooded in waves up the main street of the old town, which is now named after the unsavoury Czechoslovakian dictator, Klement Gottwald.

It was a summer's afternoon. The air had a powerful odour of melted icecream and was full of angry wasps. The trams heaved, groaned and disgorged their occupants like pregnant sows giving birth to unexpectedly large batches of piglets.

Those lucky enough to have fought for and won a seat in one of the cafés clung on to their places with murderous expressions that suggested they would physically repel all boarders, engaging in hoarse arguments with the distressed waitresses, most of whom had long since run out of icecream and were simply providing tea like the Red Cross.

I bought a guidebook to Potsdam, which made rather too much of Potsdam's noble proletarian traditions and in particular the fact that the town was once represented in the Reichstag by the left-wing Social Democrat Karl Liebknecht, who was one of the handful of German deputies to have voted against war credits in 1914. Five years later he was an associate of Rosa Luxemburg in the abortive Spartacist rising.

The former royal garrison town of the Hohenzollerns was spared the bombing that has so much altered the face of Berlin. In between the goodly sized rows of nineteenth-century mansions are humbler rows of houses built in earlier times, made of cheerful red brick and crowned by Dutch gables. It seemed a pity that Potsdam was now best known in the world for two joyless events.

The first was the service in the Garrison church on 21 March 1933. In the church where Frederick the Great was buried, Hitler sealed his triumphant accession to the chancellery in the presence of the ailing President Hindenburg and the former Crown Prince. The aged president, wearing an old fashioned *pickelhaube*, wept when Hitler declared that 'the marriage has been consumated between the symbols of the old greatness and the new strength'.

The second was the Allied conference in 1945 when the Big Three met amid the ruins of both the 'old greatness' and the 'new strength' to carve up the continent of Europe into their respective zones, leaving Germany to straddle the great ideological divide.

In a secluded park lies the mock-Tudor palace of the Cecelienhof. It was built in 1917 as a hunting lodge for Victoria's tiresome son Emperor William II and is now a luxurious hotel. The Big Three met at the Cecelienhof from 17 July to 3 August 1945 to re-draw the map of Europe and to 'authorise the transfer to Germany of German populations in Poland and Czechoslovakia'. Unfortunately, the Germany to which these 12 million refugees were sent had shrunk considerably by the time they arrived, because the same conference moved the Polish border 150 miles westwards to incorporate the historic German lands of eastern Prussia, Pomerania, Brandenburg and Silesia.

The modern reputation of Prussia as a state that was founded on philistine militarism has been a successful and enduring example of Nazi propaganda that has also been assiduously fostered by other Germans who do not care to be reminded of the fact that Nazism was founded by an Austrian and had its stronghold in Bavaria. Yet in the seventeenth and eighteenth centuries, Prussia was a model of religious tolerance and scientific enlightenment. Even after the Hohenzollerns and their allies among the 'cabbage junkers', the great landlords of the east, converted the Prussians' historic discipline into a tool for their own grandiose designs, the ordinary people of Prussia flocked in their thousands to join the most formidable Social Democratic party in Europe. Until Von Papen's unconstitutional removal of the state government in 1933, Prussia resisted the blandishments of the Nazi sirens and remained stoutly loyal to the Social Democrats. Its reward was to be abolished by the Allied council from the map of Europe in 1945 on account of its historic association with 'militarism'.

For visiting East Berliners, Potsdam is a city of French gardens and sunny palaces that recall the earlier and better days of the eighteenth century, when the young and vigorous state of Prussia was the toast of Enlightened Europe.

The smaller but the more charming of the two palaces in Potsdam is that of 'Sans Souci', a frivolous exercise in rococo set above an orangery. It was built as a summer residence for Frederick II in 1745 and finished two years later.

'The interiors meet the high and over-refined pretensions of the taste and living standards of the ruling class,' was the waspish verdict of the official guidebook. The architect, George Wencezlaus von Knobelsdorff, was a former officer in the Prussian army who resigned his commission at the age of thirty in order to qualify in architecture and painting. From there he rose rapidly and was appointed the royal superintendant of palaces and gardens. In Berlin he was responsible for the construction of the Opera and much of the façade of the Unter den Linden, with the assistance of Johann August Nahl. Frederick II spent the summer months at Sans Souci until his death in 1786. The title 'free from care' was interpreted as a snub to the theological pessimism of the Lutheran church.

The neighbouring Neue Palais was built only a few decades after the Sans Souci, but its gloomy pomposity seems to symbolise the alteration in the chemistry of Prussia that occurred around the middle of the eighteenth century. It was not designed as a royal palace at all, but as a place in which to accommodate guests of the Prussian royal family. Construction began after the end of the Seven Years' War and was completed in 1769. The vast expenditure involved, so soon after a long war, was a sign of Prussia's growing economic ascendancy over northern Germany and even over imperial Austria. The first plans for the Neue Palais were drawn up by Johann Gottfried Büring and Heinrich Manner, though in 1765 Büring was replaced by Carl von Gontard. The palace contains a great number of paintings by Italian and Dutch artists of the sixteenth to eighteenth centuries as well as a curious grotto on the ground floor.

A work that is more interesting for its documentary than artistic qualities is that of Menzel's 'coronation of Emperor William I in Königsberg in 1861'. In the front row of the church in Königsberg, which is now the city of Kaliningrad in the Soviet Union, sits Queen Victoria's daughter, 'Pussy', then Princess Victoria of Prussia and, after 1871, crown princess of Bismarck's phoney and short-lived German empire. The Machiavellian count's ghostly features hover in the background.

'Pussy' found Potsdam something of a relief from the 'dark and dreadful prison' of the Berlin Schloss, although on moving to the Neue Palais she was horrified to discover 'thousands of dead bats' in her new residence. Poor 'Pussy' made a terrible hash out of being Princess of Prussia. Nor did Prussia deserve such an intelligent and sensitive soul as its princess. For the severe and high-minded Prussia of the seventeenth and eighteenth centuries had gone as high as an old cheese. Berlin had become a vulgar caricature of its old self, given over to spivs and speculators. The air was thick with anti-semitism and the garbled nonsense of the gothic revival. The good old Prussia which had once rested content with art and science was now rummaging around in the attic, hunting for the relics of the Teutonic Knights.

Victoria was too English for the Germans and too German for the English. In Berlin she had an unfortunate habit of referring to the British navy as 'our navy', and after the Prussian war with Denmark she annoyed her brother Prince Edward in equal measure. The

Prince of Wales was married to the fragrant Alexandra of Denmark. Victoria tactlessly met both of them in Cologne with her husband Fritz, who according to Prince Edward was 'flaunting before our eyes a most objectionable ribbon' commemorating the Prussian victory over Denmark at the battle of Duppel.

The hoarse and wracking arguments between her parents-in-law distressed her (so different from the relationship between her own most perfect mama and papa), as did the coarse tittle-tattling of the Prussian courtiers and the addled anti-semitism of the court chaplains like Adolf Stöcker. These men she considered 'ambitious, narrow-minded and servile'.

In the 'stuffy, hypocritical and sham-holy Prussia' of the nineteenth-century she cut an unlikely figure. She read Dr Colenso's book on the Old Testament, dabbled in Karl Marx's *Kapital* and researched into the subject of diptheria and the possible liberation of Crete. She loathed Bismarck, who rightly feared her liberal influence on the Crown Prince and filled the Neue Palais with spies. She quarrelled also with Countess Bismarck over the subject of the bombardment of Paris in 1871. 'Pussy' was horrified by the idea, whereas the countess, true to Prussia's new swaggering spirit of bellicosity, expressed the wish that she herself could have 'thrown in firebombs shells and mortars until this accursed Sodom had been utterly destroyed'.

Raised to be a constitutional monarch and wishing only, like her mother, 'to do good', she was cheated of her role by her father-in-law living until he was ninety and then by the premature death of her husband 'Fritz' from cancer of the throat.

She was buried in the peaceful melancholy of the Friedenskirche, the 'peace church' in the grounds of the Neue Palais. This Byzantine-style church surrounds two sides of a lake with cloisters. It was built by Ludwig Persius and August Stuler and was modelled on the basilica of San Clemente in Rome.

In the apse is a mosaic which depicts Christ, John the Baptist, St Cyprian, the Mother of God and St Peter and which dates from between the tenth and twelfth centuries. Fritz's uncle, Crown Prince Frederick William, in spite of his rigid Calvinist beliefs, fell in love with it when he saw the mosaic in a church dedicated to St Cyprian near Venice and which was about to be demolished. The name Friedenskirche, the Church of Peace, was a quiet rebuke to the pagan overtones of nearby Sans Souci. In the vault lie the tombs of Frederick William VI and Queen Elizabeth Luise.

ERFURT

A fruitful Bethlehem

THEY WERE Vietnamese, in the opinion of the two men opposite me. Little men with pale delicate faces and bleached grey clothes who looked incongruous and only half incarnate next to the brightly coloured fleshiness of the Germans. I was to see them several times in the DDR and they always appeared quite disorientated by the noisy beer bars, the bulky blonde women, the heavy cream cakes and the background of spires, as if they might fade away under the competition of it all. They sat in a row in matching grey shirts and shapeless pantaloons, on the torn-up plastic seats of the Erfurt *tanzbar*. Three had passed out, leaving foaming beer glasses half consumed on the table, whilst the fourth was still hopping vaguely in time to the music on the dance floor.

'Drunk,' said the solid lad sitting opposite me.

'Ja, ja. Vietnamese drunks,' his companion added. He paused to elaborate this statement. 'Vietnamese drunks in Erfurt.'

'I think we could do better somewhere else,' the first lad added after a glass of beer tumbled off the next table on to the ground, covering us in spray and soaking the floor. He appeared to include me in this, so I nodded vigorously. 'It's a dump,' I agreed.

'Oh, I don't know. It's better here than, say, Cottbus.'

'Cottbus?'

'Ja, ja. We're from Cottbus. There's not much to do in Cottbus. Erfurt is much better.'

The Turmschenke was a small modern restaurant–cum–bar a few hundred yards down the street with a convivial air and a clientele of what Dr Johnson might have described as 'clubbable' people. 'Delighted to see you,' called out an elderly man seated with some of his companions at one of the tables on the far side of the room to the two young men as we came in. The two lads grunted sheepish greetings. 'He's a professor,' one of them whispered. 'Come and sit here,' the old man continued, shaking me by the hand.

Here indeed was a microcosm of East German society. A table designed for six, but which now groaned under the weight of a tightly packed nine. There was the elderly professor, a portly businessman who was something in cement, the two roughly spoken lads from Cottbus, a dentist who was drunk, his pretty, embarrassed wife who laughed nervously every time her husband swore at one of the waiters, a woman of uncertain years who was accompanied by her mentally disturbed son and, of course, myself. In England it could never have happened outside of wartime. The differences in social status and business occupation would have surfaced too rapidly and killed the intimacy stone dead with a thousand real and imaginary slights. Some shrill voice might have said, 'I'm in advertising', to which some gruff northern voice might have riposted, 'I'm unemployed' and the conversation would then have died a death of a thousand cuts on the barbed wire fence of the north–south divide.

But then East Germany does have the flavour of England in wartime and the atmosphere is that of the air–raid shelter in which everyone gathers in the security of the bunker without much respect for personal and social distinctions. Few can get out of Bunker DDR, and even fewer come to visit, with the result that unexpected and unchaperoned foreign guests like myself are treated to a peculiar display of awe and ignorance. 'Is it true that there are still those terrible fogs in London?' asked the dentist's wife, whose image of London appeared to have been coloured by a televised Dickensian serial.

In spite of the obvious political domination of the DDR by the Soviet Union, East Germany remains the more 'flavoursome' of the two Germanies. The smell of Germanness is more pungent in the DDR than in her western sister, in spite of all those flags proclaiming 'with the Soviet Union forever' and in spite of the half-hearted efforts of East German schools to instruct their pupils in Russian. In West Germany, much that is authentically German seems to have been suffocated by the transparent but pervasive culture of America and Pepsi Cola bottles. In the east, the Germans have been confronted by the unanswerable reality of rows of Russian tanks, but this military superiority has not been accompanied by a policy of cultural evangelism. The East Germans therefore are a great deal less 'Russianised' than the West Germans are 'Americanised'. One less positive result, however, is that the East Germans are probably less able to speak any language other than their own than any other nation in Europe, with the exception perhaps of Bulgaria or little Albania.

The East Germans have been shielded, whether they like it or not, from distractions and temptations of a fallen world. A host of modern problems afflicting the west, such as immigration, racism and the conflicts of different religions, have simply passed them by. In the fenced field of a little slice of Prussia, Brandenburg and Saxony, they have been left to ponder instead over the meaning of Germanness. Plentifully supplied with cakes, beer and contraception, the better-off East Germans have evolved a way of life that is the quintessence of *gemütlichkeit*, in such a manner that only Germans can be *gemütlich*. In the Turmschenke it became so *gemütlich* in the hot little tavern that our nine bodies seated round the table seemed to flow into one another and the conversation blended into an undulating murmur, rising and falling.

'Ja, *ja*. Bei uns in der DDR dass ist so. Ja, *ja*!'

And into our glasses the beer flowed, and it flowed, poured by the unseen hand of the waitress who refilled them unbidden and who reminded us only occasionally of her presence only by a quiet *bitte schön*.

The portly man who was something in cement announced that we were all to drink as much as we possibly could as the bill was on him, even though some of the guests at his table took to drifting off without much ceremony to other tables to chat to someone who looked interesting. The woman of uncertain years did this particularly frequently, indeed she did it every time a man over the age of twenty and under sixty appeared in the bar without any obvious company, leaving her exceedingly disorientated son to cope on his own.

I began to long for my bed in the Erfurter Hof, the large and comfortable hotel in the centre of town where the charismatic West German politician Willy Brandt had once made a triumphant appearance in front of a crowd crying 'Willy! Willy!' to the acute embarrassment of his East German host, Willy Stoph, who was well aware that the crowd were not referring to him.

'No, no, you cannot be thinking of going to bed, *now*,' said the elderly professor, 'we all need a stroll after so much beer,' and reluctantly I agreed that this was so. And so we departed from the conviviality of the Turmschenke, leaving behind the dentist who was now shouting indescribable obscenities at the waiter whilst his wife wrung her hands in humiliation. 'Pity,' said the professor. 'A very good dentist. Once upon a time!'

The four of us strolled along the street under the eaves of half-timbered houses. 'Before the war ... *after* the war, I might add, this was a wonderful town,' the professor murmured, gesticulating at the unsightly gaps in the street where several medieval houses had folded like a pack of cards through sheer neglect. 'But now ... look. No one had any money for years, you see. It has just fallen down of its own accord.' I had to agree. Poor Erfurt resembled a splendid old lady several of whose teeth had suddenly fallen out. 'Ah well. ... Just time for a nightcap, I think.'

The professor's flat was minute but immaculate – a regular bachelor pad. The two lads from Cottbus parked their large behinds on the settee and said, in unison, 'Ah ja!' Such a useful phrase, I thought, as the professor poured me a monstrously large liqueur. 'Ah ja!'

'And now for a little *translating* work, I think,' the old man said, directing a sly wink in my direction and nimbly rushing over to a small cupboard, which he then unlocked and rummaged around in as if searching for a precious object. '... now, here it is.'

'What a most delightful evening in this ancient city, that has been hallowed by the presence of the great Luther ...,' I was about to say, as a shiny magazine plopped on to my lap and my bleary eyes focused on the colourful images therein. 'What a most delight ...' was as far as I got before focusing finally on a sensational pornographic magazine that had been put together with a lurid sense of imagination that would have done justice to the paintings of Hieronymus Bosch. On each page paraded a bizarre collection of men, women and beasts encountering each other in a variety of curious positions.

'Ah *ja!*' I said. 'Ja, ja,' rejoined the two lads from Cottbus who looked at me with bovine eyes. The old professor sat himself neatly down on the sofa and shot me a penetrating, quizzical gaze. 'From America,' he said.

'Ah ja, well I can see it's not from the DDR,' I continued, still stalling. A single snigger or suppressed giggle, I realised, might send the evening spiralling off into a hazardous and regrettable course. On the other hand I didn't want to offend the two men from Cottbus, whose intentions in this affair were unknown and who were both a great deal larger than I was.

'Yeaaas now, uh.'

'Mmmm?'

'Well, I mean, there isn't really anything for me to *translate* here at all. I mean, it's all *pictures*. Isn't this kind of thing illegal in the DDR anyway?'

'Ja, ja,' agreed one of the lads. 'You can't buy it in the DDR, but everyone reads it all the same.'

'Ja, ja,' his friend agreed.

The professor snatched the magazine out of my lap, threw it back into the cupboard and stood hovering, angry and embarrassed by the door. It was, as it was so often to be during my trip, 'time to go'.

'Well, it's been very nice,' I said weakly to the two lads, who seemed quite unperturbed and merely answered. 'Ah ja.'

'Have a nice holiday in Erfurt,' I continued.

'Ja, ja,' one said, nodding. 'It's better than Cottbus.'

Erfurt reminded me of Oxford. It is a medieval city of churches and ruined monasteries, tea shops and ducks, and is populated mostly by students and the elderly. It has Oxford's clerical air, and only the sight of bicycling parsons is missing from the picture, though I dare say they are about somewhere. In the clutch of medieval churches which dot the centre of the city, Erfurters rest in the shade to eat sandwiches at lunchtime and listen to organ recitals by music students.

Much of the city remains half-timbered and cannot look altogether different today from when the young Martin Luther was ordained into the catholic priesthood in the high gothic cathedral in 1507. At that time the city was surrounded by high walls, which so impressed Luther that he believed Erfurt 'could not be taken even if it were besieged by the Turks'.

Luther's connections with the city which he styled a 'fruitful Bethlehem' were many and pleasant. It was in the relatively cosmopolitan atmosphere of Erfurt that the mind of the rough-hewn miner's son from Eisleben was irrigated by the streams of German humanism and scholasticism in the university, though he was to revolt against them and discover his own very different standpoint later on. The university of Erfurt had been founded in 1392 and was one of the oldest universities in the Holy Roman Empire, having been preceded only by Prague, Vienna, Heidelberg and Cologne. The university was unfortunately suppressed in 1816.

The Augustinian monastery at Erfurt in the early sixteenth century was a far cry from the stereotypical image of pre-reformation religious houses as asylums for dullards and drones. The Erfurt Augustinian monks had accepted the rigorous reforms promoted by the General of the Augustinian Order, Johann Staupitz, and their spiritually disciplined and academically exacting standards successfully enticed the young Luther from the lucrative secular callings his parents hoped for, into the embrace of theology and the religious life. From 1501 to 1508 he belonged to the Augustinian monastery in Erfurt, and it was here that he began to experience the peculiar anguish concerning the state of his soul that was long to torment him.

In 1508 Luther left Erfurt for the little princely court of Wittenberg where he was to join the academic staff of the town's new university. But he continued to return to Erfurt, the most celebrated occasion being when the heretical theologian from Wittenberg journeyed to the Diet of Worms to face the wrath of the Holy Roman Emperor for his attacks on the See of Rome. On his entry into Erfurt he was acclaimed as a hero by university, monastery, town council and populace alike. The Erfurters lined the streets to cheer him on his return to the Augustinian monastery.

The city authorities offered the young rebel asylum and the university held an official dinner in his honour. Back in Erfurt, Luther stayed with his old colleague at the Augustinian monastery, the abbot Johann Lang, and on the Sunday after his arrival he preached in the Augusti-

nian church. The crowds were vast, however, and so restive that
in the middle of his sermon the building appeared to be on the point
of collapse.

'Fear not,' master Luther is said to have instructed the terrified
congregation. 'That is the devil who would halt me from preaching
the gospel. But he shall not succeed!' It was fortunate for his future
reputation that the walls did not then collapse, or the entire course
of the religious history of Europe might have been altered at a stroke.

The aristocratic Council of Erfurt were wily men whose prime
aim was to safeguard their freedom of movement among the dangerous and conflicting currents in imperial politics rather than blaze a
trail for Luther's gospel. However, a little disturbance among the
citizenry and the students was useful to them as a stick with which
to browbeat the religious houses into surrendering their privileges
and to sever the ecclesiastical links that bound Erfurt to the See of
Mainz. But the council resisted avoiding committing the city exclusively to one side or the other in the subsequent religious disputes
and, in so doing, remained true to Erfurt's humanist traditions. Both
catholic and Lutheran churches remained side by side in the city and
to this day the cathedral remains Roman Catholic whilst many of
the parish churches are evangelical.

The city authorities in our own age have concocted a 'Luther trail'
to guide the inquisitive tourist from one spot in the city where Luther
said this to where he did that, but I soon abandoned this rather sterile
pilgrimage for the sheer pleasure of wandering unescorted through
Erfurt's whispering passageways and crooked alleyways, underneath
bridges, exchanging the occasional 'good morning' with one of the
many rotund Erfurt ducks waddling around the lawns and riverbanks,
for this is a watery town with many streams and riverside walks
beside which one can while away the afternoon. Like all good medieval cities, Erfurt is rich in legends, many of which connect the antics
of the legendary German alchemist of the sixteenth century Dr Faust,
or Faustus, with various houses or streets of the city. In a house
in Michaelisstrasse, for example, Dr Faustus is said to have invited
three demons to entertain his guests with rich delicacies and music.
Other stories depict him flying through the air on magic horses and
there are a host of similar escapades.

Erfurt, as the professor noted the evening before, has experienced lean times since the war. Entire streets of houses from the sixteenth and seventeenth centuries had rotted and been allowed to collapse, presumably because they had not been included in some organised and state-funded 'plan' of restoration. Over the entire city hangs a thin pall of dust, a phenomenon I was to encounter frequently in East Germany on account of the presence of unfiltered factory chimneys which have been planted near historic town centres. However, work has begun on restoring Erfurt to its old position as one of the greatest historic cities of Germany. Erfurt's famous 'Merchants' bridge', the *Kämerbrücke*, has had its half-timbered shops and houses restored, as has the market square surrounding the cathedral. The grandest merchant's house in Erfurt, the 'Hohen Lilie', is now the premier restaurant of Erfurt, in which first-class German cookery can be sampled by the diner in a suitably historic atmosphere, surrounded by portraits of eighteenth-century nobility. The Hohen Lilie belonged originally to a wealthy town councillor and goldsmith named Hiob Ludolf, whose mansion was one of the first to be built in the style of the Renaissance in Erfurt. When King Gustav Adolf of Sweden took the city in the Thirty Years' War, this became the residence of the Swedish monarch and it was also graced by the presence of his consort, Queen Eleonor, when she visited Erfurt in 1632 and was presented by the council with a Bible. The arrival of the Swedish king delighted the protestant citizenry of the city as much as it appalled the local catholics. King Gustav found them awaiting his pleasure in a state of great agitation in the Peterkloster shortly after his arrival. The king reassured them, however, that he had no intention of disturbing so much as a hair on their heads as long as they refrained from opposing him and he greeted the principal of the local Jesuits with a friendliness that was remarkable in such an age of religious strife.

At the centre of Erfurt's market square, raised up on a small hill known as the Domberg, is the great gothic cathedral of St Severus, generally known as the Erfurter Dom, a more than worthy rival to the dreaming spires of Oxford. The visitor to the cathedral is first struck by the immense fresco of St Nicholas, which is several metres high, but I was most captivated by a number of small and exquisite carvings of saints, each of which has been equipped by its anonymous medieval sculptor with a most striking quality of personality. All the genius of the medieval craftsmen of the old high Germany of the Middle Ages seemed invested in these magnificent tiny sculptures, whose plastic limbs curved and twisted as happened to take the sculptor's seemingly effortless fancy. They made contemporary English sculptures, those which survived the mindless iconoclasm of our reformation, seem stiff and lifeless in comparison.

Erfurt is a city of cafés, as are all the best student cities. Although the number of tourists in Erfurt is small, these cafés are always full of natives, which renders queueing for a seat inevitable in all but the most expensive. In order to secure a place, therefore, I had to adapt my daily schedule so as to eat at twelve, dine at six and so forth, in order to avoid the twice-daily rush hours.

The East Germans are, as it were, all dressed up but with nowhere to go. With money in their pockets, or more money than anyone else in the eastern bloc at any rate, they have been denied the opportunity to fritter it away in the kind of manner we are accustomed to in the west. Few outside the country villages live in private accommodation and the state rents are extremely cheap. Expensive foreign holidays are difficult to come by and expeditions to the west, other than those covered by 'urgent family business', as the official phrase goes, are few and far between. A limited number of package holidays are available to Cuba and the Soviet Union and other approved countries, but even these are far fewer than the number wanting to go.

'You can get turned down if they don't like the shape of your nose,' a young nurse from Erfurt told me over *Kaffee und Kuchen*. 'They don't have to give you a reason for not letting you on holiday.'

The young nurse's solution, so she said, was to go to Berlin every weekend, where she would dress up in her finest clothes and glide confidently into the lobby of the most expensive hotels posing as a West German tourist. Once there, she could illegally exchange her East German marks for hard currency, which she hoped to use in purchasing a ticket to Munich, where she had a girl friend.

For those who are not interested in wasting their marks or exchanging them at a prohibitive rate for western currency, there is only one answer. Spend, spend, spend, on the few things you can really blow your money on, of which the most obvious is food and entertainment. In consequence, the restaurants and cafés of the DDR bulge under the weight of 16 million East Germans eating furiously through their unspent cash, with cakes and burgers, steaks and chickens, coffees and liqueurs, icecreams and torten, beers and cocktails ... one is reminded immediately of Katherine Mansfield's sharp observations of the German obsession with matters digestary in *In a German Pension*.

And drinking. The East Germans are not reduced to courting oblivion with poisonous fire waters and lethal vodkas. They soak themselves luxuriantly in a rich and splendid array of beers, coffees made with mocca and brandy, and cocktails floating in cream, all of which are available almost round the clock, as the pubs have never suffered from the same kind of licensing laws that we have laboured under in England. They are the Americans of eastern Europe in their nervous obsession with packing in as much calorie intake per day as possible and ensuring that at no point in their lives will they miss out on a meal. For even when they go for country walks, they travel in organised groups on carefully laid trails lined every four hundred yards or so with an 'Imbiss' snackery, in order that the stomach should never suffer from lack of a Frankfurter or a *strudel*.

The Café Rommel in Leninstrasse, Erfurt, was the most delightful afternoon establishment I found in East Germany. Leninstrasse was not, as its name suggested, a five-lane boulevard lined with Stalinist monuments, but a dear little half-timbered avenue in the historic centre of Erfurt and which in England would have rejoiced under the name 'Duck Lane' or 'The Shambles', but which the East German authorities had renamed Leninstrasse in a fit of misguided doctrinal enthusiasm. Nothing appeared to have altered in the dark waxed wooden interior of the Café Rommel for at least forty years, neither the old till, nor the large wooden wireless which burbled inconsequentially and soothingly in the background, nor indeed the old waitress in starched hat and pinny going calmly about her business. Students chattered in one corner, old Erfurt ladies in another, the one group exchanging whispered confidences, the other shouting at each other at the top of their voices about which type of cake they should order. And it was here in the Café Rommel that several afternoons in Erfurt melted effortlessly away in a haze of hot buttered toast, tea and rustling newspapers.

WITTENBERG

Gloriosa Dei civitas

> From here went out the call to the guests, let them
> come, let them come. And they came from every
> country, state and people, Italians, Frenchmen,
> Spaniards and Portuguese, Britons and Scots,
> Scandinavians from the North Sea, but also Poles,
> Hungarians and southern Slavs, yes even from the
> Balkans and the Caucasus they came . . . .
>
> *Giordano Bruno on Wittenberg*

THEY ALSO CAME from Vietnam, judging from their matching grey
boiler suits. They were standing at the taxi rank outside Wittenberg
railway station looking heart-breakingly lost.

'Witt?' one of them asked.

'Ja, Witt,' I answered reassuringly. The woman queueing behind
me in the taxi rank eyed their boiler suits and Asiatic faces with
suspicion.

The Vietnamese handed me the crumpled piece of paper he had
been holding in his hand. Underneath a mass of Asiatic hieroglyphics
were written three words:

Dres. 16. Witt.

It was not a lot to go on. 'Hmm,' I said. 'This could be Number
16, Dresdener strasse, Wittenberg.'

'I hope it isn't Number 16 Wittenberg strasse, Dresden,' commented the woman behind me. She evidently hoped that it was.

I gave this woman a cold, reproving look for her unsolicited advice and led the little fellow over to a map of the town of Wittenberg inside the station waiting room.

'Stadtplan!' I announced, trying to invest the word with as much significance as possible. 'Now, ... here we are. Dresdener strasse! See? Off you go.' The two little men trotted off into the distance on errands unknown.

'We have *meat* in Wittenberg,' confided the receptionist at the Hotel Golden Eagle where I had lodgings, '... and, we have *cake*.' The receptionist was a motherly woman, given to whispered confidences, who eyed my comings and goings with proprietorial concern. She was almost a perfect sphere in shape, with sparrow legs and a large head that rested on rather than grew out of the flesh beneath.

I was drunk, beguiled by cheap cocktails and waitresses who smelt of a heady concoction of beer, cigarette smoke and perfume as they refilled my glass with a softly spoken 'bitte schön'.

'... we have all these things in plenty in Wittenberg,' the receptionist continued. I swung unsteadily around the large wooden banisters of the staircase beside the desk, from which as far as I could tell, she never moved.

'... but spare parts for automobiles and things like *that*, never! Why only last week a couple drove down here from Berlin, a nice couple, dentists I believe, and their car broke down. I don't know exactly what it was they needed, but there was no finding it here. They had to go *back* to Berlin by *train*, find the spare parts and then return to Wittenberg the following weekend to collect the car.'

'What a pair of fools,' I half shouted (yes, I was definitely drunk). The receptionist looked at me archly, as if to suggest that it was way past my bedtime.

The 'Protestant Rome' was a disappointing sight. Wittenberg was neither the glorious city of God nor the turreted German Oxford of my imagination. There was not a great deal which hinted at the glory which was Wittenberg's, when the city was the residence of the Electors of Saxony and the seat of a great university. Not to mention the meteor-like brilliance of the early years of the reformation, when Martin Luther's thunderous missives to the German nation nearly succeeded in toppling the papal tiara.

Two long dusty streets, lined with grainy-looking shop windows displaying things no one could possibly want to buy, straggled from the Castle church to the Black Monastery, passing a fine town hall built in the style of the renaissance and an imposing parish church. And that was that. As I walked up College Street I had an uneasy feeling that the Berlin Wall, for all its armed guards, alsatians, barbed wire and death traps, was more of a metaphor than a reality. The real Wall lay unseen in some innocent field on the way between Berlin and the dull, undulating Saxon countryside. I had crossed it without even knowing it, absorbed in reading *Neues Deutschland* on the train.

By an Imperial Golden Bull of 1356, Wittenberg became the residence of the new Duchy of Saxony. In 1423 the Duchy of Saxony was divided between two branches of the Wettin family, the so-called 'Ernestine' and 'Albertine' branches. Wittenberg fell to the Ernestines. Wittenberg was still only a small ducal residence, however, when the most illustrious of the Ernestine Wettins, Frederick the Wise, founded a university to adorn his court in 1502.

The new university rapidly achieved eminence, or notoriety, depending upon one's convictions, as a centre for the new 'humanist' thinking. The university was much influenced by the works of scholars of international reputations like Erasmus, who were openly deriding the more extravagant papal claims as fraudulent and ridiculing the old orthodoxies of the church.

Six years after the foundation of the new university in Wittenberg, a new professor of theology was appointed. He was a young Augustinian monk, aged twenty-nine and not long since priested in the great cathedral at Erfurt. He was a great admirer of Erasmus and his name was Martin Luther.

If the reformation can be said to have begun in one single place, it was in Wittenberg's Castle church. The present Castle church at the end of College Street is largely the work of nineteenth-century restorers, who descended on the town after Wittenberg was absorbed into the kingdom of Prussia in 1815 and who were determined to create monuments to Luther's personal influence on the town. On the high wooden tower of the Castle church they engraved the words which can be seen from miles away, 'Ein feste Burg ist unser Gott.'

The young theology professor at Wittenberg had begun to dabble in dangerous thoughts, thoughts which had led his Bohemian predecessor Jan Huss to the stake at Constance a century earlier. Martin Luther's anguished studies of the Pauline Epistles, in particular the letter of St Paul to the Romans, had imbued him with an extraordinary, terrifying revelation. The teaching of the Roman church, the barque of Peter, on the means of salvation was incorrect.

Man was not saved by the performance of good 'works' and in particular by the sacrificial 'work' of the Mass, as the Roman church taught, but by 'faith alone' in the grace of God, which was predestined from the beginning of time to His Elect.

Such talk might have ended as nothing more than an academic squabble in the universities, which thrived on such abstract philosophical discussions about faith and salvation. It was certainly way beyond the heads of the mass of the peasants. The normal course of such affairs was a flurry of letters between the authorities in Rome and the relevant secular prince. The prince would waver in his resolve. The Roman authorities would concede a few privileges over the appointments of abbots and suchlike. The heretic and his books would then be burnt in the courtyard of the royal palace in front of a fidgety assembly of bishops, royal personages and uncomprehending peasants, or alternatively the miscreant would merely be dispatched to an obscure marshland parish. Either way peace would return to the vineyard. At worst, as in the case of the fourteenth-century English heretic John Wycliffe, his ideas would spawn an irritating anti-clerical sect among the more rebellious artisans of the towns.

The remorseless mind of the Augustinian monk, however, did not stop short at these academic conclusions but moved irrresistibly to new elucidations. And these, with the aid of Luther's unrivalled mastery of the rolling cadences of the German language and the newly invented printing presses, he was able to communicate to the whole of Germany.

The sale of indulgences by a preacher called Tetzel was a harmless enough affair. The papal court was costly to maintain. The great church of St Peter's needed rebuilding. Let the furrowed brows of the peasants be ironed out by releasing them of their sins for a small fee!

The prices charged by the itinerant indulgence seller for the remission of sins shed an interesting light on contemporary attitudes towards crime. Sodomy commanded a hefty twelve ducats, murder but seven, bigamy six and sorcery a paltry two. The sale was a glaring example of the corruption of Christian faith that stemmed from the doctrine of salvation by 'works' and it became the occasion of a great howl from Martin Luther against the onerous clutter of late medieval catholic dogma. On 31 October 1517 Luther posed certain questions to the university, to Rome and to Germany in 'Ninety-Five Theses'. These he nailed to the doors of the Castle church.

The essence of the theses was that the priesthood was not the property of the clergy but of all Christian believers. Here was news that could be grasped by the most simple and uneducated peasant.

If all men were priests, what need for the great abbeys and princely bishoprics and their tyrannous extortions? If salvation could not be 'earned' by the prayers of the faithful, but depended on God's freely given grace, what need for the massed ranks of cowled monks, with their troublesome exemptions from the civil laws and duties that fell on laymen? If man needed no intercessor between his soul and the grace of God, what need of confession? Of bishops? Or indeed of the pope?

The 'Ninety-Five Theses' created a sensation throughout Germany within days of their being pinned to the doors of the Castle church in Wittenberg. This alone ought to have ensured Luther's speedy despatch to the stake. But Germany had changed since the days of Jan Huss. The *burgermeisters* of the towns were hungry for the wealth of the abbeys and monasteries within their walls. In the eyes of some of the princes, the rebel monk was a useful bargaining point in their dealings with the Holy Roman Emperor. Moreover Luther had a firm ally at the court of the Elector of Saxony in George Spalatin, the Elector's chaplain.

The orthodoxy of the universities had been diluted by the academic ferment of humanistic study. Had not Erasmus himself, the licensed jester of the papal court, been castigating the pretensions of popes, monks and the clergy for years with impunity? Deep in the German countryside the enserfed peasantry sniffed the wind of the commotion in the towns and prepared to rise against the abbots and prince bishops.

In 1520, the bull 'Exsurge Domine' gave Martin Luther sixty days to recant his heresies. Luther replied by burning the bull in front of Wittenberg's 'Magpie Gate'. Throughout 1521 Luther remained in hiding in the Wartburg castle in Eisenach, but in 1522 he staged a triumphant return to Wittenberg under the protection of the Elector.

There was much to be done. Wild spirits had emerged in Wittenberg in Luther's absence. A radical preacher named Thomas Muntzer took Luther's word on the 'priesthood of all believers' to mean that all men should be equal on the earth as well as in heaven. Such language was distressing to the Elector, not to mention the effect it was having on the Leviathan of the peasantry. Luther found a responsible figure in John Bugenhagen to oversee the work of the reformation in Wittenberg parish church.

The parish church of St Mary's lies behind a row of merchants' houses in the town hall square. These merchants' houses reflect the prosperity of Wittenberg in the golden years of the mid-sixteenth century, when through the fame of its illustrious preacher, the university blossomed and the town became a centre for publishing Bibles, which attracted merchants, artisans and artists.

The most illustrious of these artists was Lucas Cranach the Elder, who arrived in Wittenberg in 1505 and remained there for the next forty-five years. Aside from his skills in painting, he was a prominent civic dignitary in the town, serving as Wittenberg's *Burgermeister* on several occasions in the 1530s and 1540s.

The exterior of St Mary's church is decorated with the worn funerary monuments of seventeenth-century Saxon ladies, their faces almost entirely obscured from public gaze by voluminous cloaks, veils and tall hats.

The interior of the church contains several fine works of art from the age when John Bugenhagen was pastor of Wittenberg, for the Lutheran reformation, unlike its Calvinist counterpart in England, promoted instead of suppressing the old tradition of ecclesiastical art.

The altarpiece, begun by Lucas Cranach the Elder and completed by his son, reveals the intimate links between the great figures of the reformation and the town in which they lived and loved. The central panel shows Luther preaching the doctrine over a figure of the crucified Christ to an audience which included his wife, the former nun Katherine von Bora. Another panel shows the new evangelical communion service being celebrated in a company of contemporary citizens of Wittenberg which include the town pastor, John Bugenhagen. Another panel depicts a service of baptism. The baptism is being conducted by Luther's colleague, Melancthon. Melancthon was a renowned theologian and the author of the new evangelical church's statement of faith, the 'Augsburg Confession'. But he was also a layman. The choice of Melancthon as the agent of baptism, therefore, was a lesson to the parishioners of Wittenberg in the implications of the 'priesthood of all believers'.

The epitaph to Paul Eber by Cranach the Younger, entitled *The Vineyard of the Lord* is a great example of the polemical passion aroused by the reformation. On the left side, popes, bishops, priests and monks destroy the vineyard of the Lord by tearing up the vines. On the right side, Luther, Melancthon and Bugenhagen tend the vines and burn the weeds.

The painting is a striking reminder of how Luther divided Germany into ideologically hostile zones in a manner that foretold the division of Germany after the Second World War, for the Lutherans, like the communists who assumed power in the DDR after 1949, were not content with merely overseeing their own reformation. They insisted on painting their opponents in the vilest colours. That the pope was not merely in error, but the antichrist, was an article of faith for which Luther was personally responsible. The gentle and mediating figure of Erasmus, upon whose word Luther once hung with dogged devotion, was not spared Luther's choleric denunciations either, for he refused to choose between the twin poles of Wittenberg and Rome and died despised by partisans of both sides.

The Black Monastery lies at the other end of College Street from the Castle Church. In 1525 Luther married Katherine von Bora and on the first floor of the former monastery the two of them constructed the family home. The monastery is now a museum of the reformation and the largest museum of that kind in the world. The interior of the monastery has altered much over the centuries, but the 'Lutherstube', where Luther, now the patriarch of the reformed churches, held much of his celebrated 'table talk' with visiting students, remains in its original form. Over the doorway one can still make out the scrawled signature of Peter the Great.

Outside this snug chamber, however, hangs a large polemical nine-teenth-century painting, which portrays the beginning of the era of disasters that befell the city of Wittenberg after Luther's death. The painting depicts the Duke of Alba in the company of an unpleasant-looking cardinal, who is urging him to disinter the grave of Martin Luther from the chancel of the Castle Church.

Within a year of Luther's burial in the Castle church in 1546, Witten-berg reaped a harvest of misfortunes. The 'Schmalkaldik' League of protestant princes was defeated by the catholic forces of the Holy Roman Emperor, Charles V, and the city of Wittenberg fell to the imperial army. The emperor robbed Wittenberg of its privileged position as the seat of the 'Ernestine' Dukes of Saxony and it became part of 'Albertine' Saxony, whose dukes held court in Dresden.

Melancthon remained in Wittenberg until his death in 1560, but Wittenberg was rapidly losing its importance as the centre of protestant theology. The very ease by which the reformation had succeeded in Wittenberg under the protection of the Saxon Electors induced a certain theological moderation and complacency. After Melancthon's death, the intellectual joints in the university began to seize up. In England, Scotland, France and the Netherlands, protestant reformers wrestled with hostile and persecuting princes. Their eyes turned naturally towards the more militant and dynamic theology that was emerging from Calvin's academy in Geneva.

The academic decline of the university and the loss of the city's political status was accompanied by economic decline. The town was badly damaged by the Swedish army during the Thirty Years' War and in 1637 it was swept with plague. Further destruction occurred during the Seven Years' War from 1756 to 1763, when much of the remaining fabric was destroyed by the Prussians. The town suffered yet another invasion in 1806, when it was occupied by the French. On a single day, 20 October 1806, the French army consumed 6,000 bottles of wine and 30,000 rations of bread, all of which had to be supplied by the citizens of Wittenberg. The once great university which in 1520 housed 20,000 students now contained a paltry 50 and in 1817 came the final humiliation when the university was amalga-mated into the university of Halle.

Four and a half centuries after Luther's reformation in Wittenberg, I discovered little love lost between the town's catholics and protestants.

I asked the bird-like attendant in the Black Monastery about the polemical picture of the Duke of Alba standing over Luther's grave.

'An unpleasant picture,' I commented.

'Oh, I don't know,' she said briskly. 'I am catholic myself and no fan of Luther's.'

'How curious that you work in the Luther museum!'

'Job ist Job,' she said, heavily.

'Well I'm interested to hear there is a catholic community in the so-called "Protestant Rome".'

'I would not call it "a community". There is a small diaspora of catholics from the Sudetenland in Czechoslovakia like me, who came here after the war.'

There was no pleasing her, even when I added hopefully that I had heard much about the work of the Cardinal Archbishop in Berlin.

'Really?' she said. 'I have heard nothing about him at all. In Wittenberg we are under the jurisdiction of the Bishop of Passau in the Federal Republic.'

'So the German catholic church remains a symbol of German unity,' I insisted desperately.

She drew herself up for one last scold. 'The catholic church is not "German". It stretches from one end of the world to the other!'

'Everything goes to Berlin' is a complaint never far from the lips of disgruntled Saxons and Thuringians in East Germany. There is certainly very little to do in Wittenberg in the evenings except watch the swallows and pigeons wheeling and coursing around the tower of the castle church in the evening sunset.

There was only one restaurant which had hoisted itself from the spit and sawdust of the beer *stubes*, which was situated in the cellar of the Castle church. Although I arrived by seven o'clock, I discovered to my dismay that there was already a long queue outside the door. A girl in front of me, who was waiting for her friend, chattered on in a tone of didactic affability.

'I think everyone should have a boy or girl friend. It is just not right to be alone, don't you think?'

'In our DDR schools, catholics, protestants and atheists like myself all learn to tolerate and respect each other's beliefs, which is, of course, absolutely correct,' etc, etc.

She said she hoped that an English pop-star called Billy Idol would one day visit Wittenberg. I told her I knew of one person who had committed suicide by throwing herself out of a window after listening to Billy Idol too often. She was not put off by this information.

'I can well believe it,' she said. 'He is a real devil.'

The manager appeared at last, though he was obviously drunk. He gave us all a mocking glance, and from behind the glass panels of the door stuck up two fingers in an unmistakable V sign. He then slapped his thighs in silent laughter and left. The queue of people shuffled silently in the darkness. Quite disheartened, I left.

On the way back to the Golden Eagle I was stopped in College Street by a sad-looking couple in their 30s.

'Do you know the way to the cabaret?' they asked. I was amazed that Wittenberg ran to something as exotic as a cabaret, so I asked to accompany them.

We located the amateur theatre in a post-war social hall, where along with the bourgeoisie of Wittenberg we dined at our small tables in front of the stage.

The couple spent much of their time sighing.

'So you come from England?' (sigh).

'I went to visit my mother in Bonn once, but my wife wasn't allowed to accompany me' (sigh).

'... yes, we're both doctors. Oh yes, we are very well paid by DDR standards. But the salaries are nothing compared to those in the Federal Republic' (sigh).

There was no cheering them, though I tried to mollify their depression with tales of storms in England that had uprooted whole villages, with plagues in Spain, riots in France and with hastily invented but suitably horrifying statistics about mugging in New York.

They looked gloomier than ever. They were not remotely interested in comparisons between East Germany and England or France. Their expectations revolved around an imaginary axis running between the two sides of Germany. West Germany was the subject of their hopes and longings and also of the object of their divided feelings.

'At least your mother made it to Bonn,' I concluded hopefully.

'Oh, she's terribly unhappy in Bonn,' the husband assured me. 'If she had the choice she would come back, but of course she is not allowed to' (sigh).

The play was a bedroom farce about a young couple staying in their parents' flat. The two of them had purchased a strange electrically operated divan which folded into the wall to make extra living space during the daytime. Each time they attempted making love, however, they were interrupted by the unexpected arrival of grandma, or their parents wanting to pass through the living room, or by a friendly neighbour calling in for a chat. It was a parody and probably a not inaccurate one of the pains and pleasures of life in the DDR, of all its friendliness and matiness and of the cramped feeling of an exuberant nation constrained within the walls of tiny flats and the walls of a small country.

I felt free to laugh when the electric divan blew a fuse and the entire bed exploded. The faces of my sad friends, for whom the tale had a ring of truth beyond the exaggerated farce, scarcely moved a muscle.

QUEDLINBURG

The Harz Mountains

WITTENBERG WAS a great deal smaller than Berlin, though even in the East German capital my solitary travels were regarded with a mixture of admiration and apprehension. 'You are on holiday in East Germany on your own?' I was often asked. 'Why have you come for a holiday here?'

Quedlinburg was a great deal smaller than Wittenberg, however. So no little stir was caused by the arrival of a solitary Englishman pulling a suitcase on wheels behind him into the hall-way of the hotel 'Quedlinburg Hof'. A waiter who I discovered was Bulgarian immediately appeared. So did the restaurant waitress. She was soon followed by the middle-aged manageress of the Quedlinburg Hof who looked flustered as she fiddled nervously with a string of fake pearls around her neck. It was clearly all very exciting, but at the same time distressing. The East Germans do not like to be distressed. Quedlinburg above all was unused to disturbing novelties.

My passport was examined carefully. 'English!' I felt the manageress would have used the same tone if she had exclaimed instead 'Martian!' Each page was examined to ensure that all was in order and that the requirements of the East German state had in no way been infringed. The manageress donned a pair of horn-rimmed glasses in order better to scrutinise my hotel voucher. It unmistakeably stated that the East German tourist authorities had afforded the bearer permission to travel without let or hindrance in the town of Quedlinburg.

'You had better go to the police station,' concluded the manageress. She was evidently still unwilling to shoulder the sole responsibility of my disturbing presence within Quedlinburg. The Bulgarian waiter nodded in agreement. 'Just to register. To be sure.'

Quedlinburg police station was situated in a nineteenth-century villa, shrouded by overgrown rhododendrons. I knocked and entered through the hallway into a room where a well built policewoman was sitting behind a desk. A thatch of blonde hair protruded from her small peaked cap.

'May I come in? I wish to register.'

'You may not,' she shouted. 'Go back outside and push your passport through the letterbox.'

I walked back outside the room, closed the door and pushed my passport through the letterbox. It landed with a soft plop. Seconds later I could hear the chair being scraped back and heavy footsteps advancing towards the door.

'Come in!' I re-entered. The policewoman handed me back my passport. 'Everything is in order. You may go.'

At the Quedlinburg Hof a terribly dreary wedding party was taking place in the restaurant. There were about fifteen guests seated at a trestle table in absolute silence in a corner of the room. I sat down at a table near the wedding party and smiled timidly. No one smiled back. The bride drummed her fingers on the table-top; the bride's mother appeared to be engaged in counting the number of cracks on the ceiling; the groom smoked what looked like his hundredth cigarette of the day; all around a sepulchral collection of relatives fingered the stems of their wine glasses. Whoever talks about the gay frivolity of continental weddings, I decided, has evidently not visited the German Democratic Republic.

The Bulgarian waiter, in a kind of macabre diversion, was dancing in attendance round the trestle table, cracking jokes and being ignored by everyone. The waitress fiddled quietly away with the old gramophone in the opposite corner and then startled the life out of us all by suddenly playing, very loudly, an English pop song called 'Life is Life'. It was an inappropriate record to be played at the Quedlinburg Hof.

The East German capital has not been infected by the lethargy that is common to public servants in other eastern bloc countries. It is held at bay by native Prussian tradition and the teasing presence of West Berlin on the other side of the Wall. Most restaurants and hotels are state-owned and tips are by no means *de rigeur*. The waiters and waitresses therefore have no vested interest in serving anyone at all. But in Berlin they do and frequently with an unaccountable smile on their faces. Away from the capital, however, without the stimulus of impatient western tourists, the joints seize up a little; the ritual of waiting becomes a little ossified.

After ten minutes of having sat unserved at my table in the Quedlinburg Hof, therefore, I asked the waitress why I had not yet received a menu.

'Because you have not been seated,' she said. 'You sat down yourself.' She spoke more in sorrow than in anger, so I went off and found the Bulgarian waiter. He agonised over where I should be seated, although the room was entirely empty apart from the trestle table occupied by the wedding party. At last he found a seat that corresponded to his satisfaction and mine. I then asked him for a menu.

'You must ask the waitress for a menu,' he said. 'I am responsible for seating.' Although he would not bring me a menu, however, he darted across the floor at great speed to light my cigarette the second I placed it in my mouth.

The waitress produced a menu listing several tempting dishes. After no more than a few seconds, however, she removed it from the table and replaced it with a small white card on which was engraved in gothic letters 'The Quedlinburg Hof recommends'. Underneath was written in pencil the single word 'Pork'.

When she returned I said, 'I think I will go for the pork.'

Quedlinburg is an ancient town, a child's dream of the crooked, mysterious and faintly sinister old Germany of the Grimms' tales. It is the kind of town in which one imagines that walking widdershins around the church tower would result in being bound by goblins and transported to a faery castle underneath a mountain. The houses nearly all date from the sixteenth or seventeenth centuries. They are higher than their English counterparts, with brightly painted diamond-shaped wooden cornices. Many are engraved with the date of their construction and those rhyming couplets beloved by the loquacious Germans of the high Middle Ages, such as:

Anno Christi 1577. Martin Huener.
In Gottes gewalt habe ich gestalt.

In most East German towns the authorities have planted, perhaps as an act of faith in the proletariat, a large boot factory or a cement works. From their unfiltered chimneys emerges an immense quantity of smoke and soot. It is this that gives many East German towns the appearance of having had a bucket of ash emptied over them. Were Quedlinburg in England, the spell of the past would have been broken by different means. Public toilets, Olde Worlde Tea Shoppes, souvenir stalls and huge car parks would have been erected to accommodate the summer crowds of tourists.

Quedlinburg has avoided both these fates. Old Germany dozes undisturbed. The occasional hitch-hiker snoozes under the spreading branches of the large oaks in the churchyards, ignored by bumble bees performing the afternoon chores of collecting pollen from the wild flowers that grow profusely in the long grass. Old ladies lean out of their brightly painted window sills to watch and wait for something to happen; for a cat to jump, or a child to clatter through the cobbled streets on his bicycle.

The public buildings of Quedlinburg bear witness to the pride of this early medieval town, before the rising power of the princes, fresh from successful battles of wills with the Holy Roman Emperors, blighted its aspiration of civic independence. In the centre of the town is a fine castle set high upon a hill, wherein lie the tenth-century tombs of Duke Henry I and his consort Mathilda. There is an old town hall from the fourteenth century, with the arms of the Quedlinburg eagle embellished over the doorway.

The tale of Quedlinburg is the tale of many German towns. It bloomed in the twelfth-century renaissance and was cut down in the fifteenth. Ironically, it was the destruction of Quedlinburg's independence in the fifteenth century which gave the town its petrified beauty. Quedlinburg's arrested development preserved it from the corruption of adulthood, like Sleeping Beauty.

In 1179, Quedlinburg already possessed city walls, the hallmark

of a *burgerlich* community with aspirations to be rid of princely thrall-
dom. The town began to split into two parts. Quedlinburg proper,
which clustered around the castle, the 'Burg'; and a new foundation
called 'Neustadt' centred around the market place now occupied by
'Mathilda's Fountain'. The new town possessed its own town hall,
which was subsequently destroyed in the Thirty Year's War, and
its own parish churches.

Eight medieval churches from the twelfth and thirteenth centuries
survive from this highpoint in Quedlinburg's prosperity. The twin
spires of St Nicholas in Neustadt are still the most arresting sight
in the town. St Nicholas was built in 1201, financed perhaps by a
wealthy shepherd, for amongst the statues on the church tower is
a shepherd with his dog. Inside is a small statue of Bishop Godehard
of Hildesheim holding a reliquary. The church enjoys some fame
from the life of Johann Christian Erxleben, pastor of St Nicholas
from 1735 to 1759 and whose wife Dorothea Christiane graduated
as the first woman doctor in Germany from the university of Halle
in 1754.

Many of the other churches in Quedlinburg are unfortunately in
the most lamentable condition, though the Market church contains
a splendid pulpit.

In the fifteenth century Quedlinburg over-reached itself. The city
applied for membership of the Hanseatic League, an association of
independent mercantile city states. Such fully fledged independence
could not be maintained against the Wettin branch of the Duchy
of Saxony, whose dukes forced the town to surrender its privileges
and henceforth did their utmost to stifle the town's development
by restricting the construction of new houses. So Quedlinburg
remained a town built in wood rather than stone in which little was
built and little fell down. Quedlinburg still contains the oldest house
in East Germany, a fine round whitewashed house from 1350.

There was an old Dresdener among our party who toured the town.
I had noticed him at the breakfast table in the Quedlinburg Hof.
He must have been eighty years old at least, though his thick bristle
of white hair and vigorous manner concealed the passage of the years.
I assumed he was an East German. As I had slipped into the East
German habit of referring to everything by initials – DDR for East

Germany; BRD for West Germany; CSSR for Czechoslovakia, and so on – I simply turned to him and enquired, 'DDR or BRD?'

'Don't give me that BRDDDR business,' he replied. 'What is wrong with the word *German*?'

The old man liked to interrupt our tour with jocose observations. 'The fruits of capitalism!' he once remarked as our guide droned on gently about a row of merchants' houses in front of us. He liked to remind us that although he came from Dresden, he now resided in the west. 'Now that house reminds me of some of our old parts of Munich,' he would say. The rest of the party raised their eyes in exasperation. They had neither visited Munich nor enjoyed any likelihood of doing so before they were old age pensioners.

When the tour was over, I went for a beer in the old half-timbered pub, the 'Schlosskrug am Dom', on top of the hill outside the castle. I looked down over the pitched red roofs of Quedlinburg, over the silver-grey buns of the old ladies leaning motionless over their window-sills, and remembered a line from Stevie Smith's poems: 'Dreaming Germany, with your urge and your might. . . .'

'It's a scandal don't you think?'

I started. It was the old Dresdener. He sat down at my table with a large foaming lager in his hand. 'Have you seen the state of some of these buildings? Really these people are as poor as church mice.'

I sighed and nodded my head in agreement. There cannot be more than half a dozen towns in East Germany that are blessed with so many small pearls of medieval German architecture as Quedlinburg. Beyond the meticulously restored centre of the town, however, an entire quarter containing several streets and an old church had been allowed to fall to pieces. Quedlinburg lies close to the frontier with West Germany. For some months following the end of the war it became part of the territory of the American zone of occupation, before being handed over to the Russians. Perhaps the departing Americans were accompanied by a good many citizens of Quedlinburg. Whatever happened, this quarter of old streets was deserted. The roof of the church was open to the sky. Shrubs had sprouted from the window frames and collapsed rafters of the houses, most of which had long passed the point of possible restoration.

I dreaded returning to the Quedlinburg Hof that evening in case the wedding party was still there in the restaurant. I had a horrible vision of discovering them there all dead and slumped over the trestle table whilst the record player in the corner continued to blare 'Life is Life'.

Instead I discovered the smartest restaurant in town, the 'Buntes Lamm'. No sooner had I passed through the doorway than I realised that the Buntes Lamm had been redecorated in the same, somewhat oppressive, 'Prussian boudoir' style as so many other restaurants in Berlin. The restaurant was overwhelmingly pink. There were corn dollies on pink walls. Tiny pink tables, which had been designed to be knocked over as easily as possible, were laden with pink candles, flowers and frilly napkins. The waitress was pink, except her teeth and hair, which were both a jaundiced shade of yellow. I suspected that the food she would serve would also be pink.

The carpet was a deep pink pile. I swam cautiously back towards the door, but not before the waitress swam out to intercept me from the alcove in which she had been waiting, bearing a menu.

I was trapped.

There is one of these deadly establishments in every town in East Germany; a restaurant that has been elevated to a level of such stifling propriety that the customers are reduced to an awed silence. Only the most daring conduct furtive conversations in whispers. I knew that dinner in the Buntes Lamm would reduce me to the same kind of hysteria I once experienced in a similar restaurant in Erfurt, where I found the silence so threatening that I was seized by an urge, almost but fortunately not entirely irresistible, to remove my clothes and dance naked on the table. The waitress came to take my order, but the thought of my whispered request, 'Pork chop, please', echoing around the silent restaurant was somehow so unbearably amusing that I began to shake and shudder with muffled snorts of suppressed laughter. I remembered how the waitress had stood there with the note-book in her hand whilst I attempted several times and without success to utter the simple phrase 'pork chop, please' without laughing. When helpless tears began to roll down my cheeks, I stuffed the beautifully folded table napkin in my mouth to stifle my sobs. The waitress then gave up in disgust and I felt compelled to leave the restaurant without delay. I did not want the same episode to recur in the Buntes Lamm so I handed the menu smartly back to the waitress and left.

The seedy and smoke-filled gloom of the Tanzbar Quedlinburg was more comfortable. Around the walls, Quedlinburg's less affluent citizens were gazing hopefully at the young show-girls boogying on the dance floor. On one table a woman in her fifties with her hair in a bun, much like any of the ladies I had seen gazing over their window-sills and watching the world go by, was sitting opposite a couple much younger than herself.

A teenage blade sauntered over to her table with a cracked smile and, after exchanging a few sly winks with his mates, asked the grey-haired lady to dance. 'I hope she boxes your ears, you insolent young puppy,' I thought. I was quite wrong. She stubbed out her cigarette, looked at the young couple sitting opposite her as if to say, 'Just watch me!' and then steered her young partner through a vigorous rock'n'roll on the dance floor.

The grand old Dresdener insisted on giving me a lift as far as Halle, whence I could catch a train to Weimar. He informed me over breakfast in the Quedlinburg Hof that he was driving back to Munich. He had only stopped for two days in Quedlinburg on the way back from Dresden, which city he visited each year to see old friends and relations.

I sat at the breakfast table with an East German woman, who told us she had been born in Riga. What a mobile and restless tide the Germans are, I thought, forever lapping at the corners of Europe then retreating back where they came from. The old Dresdener boomed away.

'The first time I came back was in the autumn of 1945. There was no way I could cross into the Russian zone so what did I do? I dressed up as a railway worker and slipped in on a goods train.'

The woman from Riga looked impressed. She opened her mouth, no doubt in order to slip in a few tales of her own escape from Riga, but the old Dresdener had only just started.

'My mother told me: "You stay right where you are. Don't come back here." She knew how things would turn out in the Russian zone. She died in 1950. I went back last year to put some flowers on her grave. Do you know what they had done? They had taken away the tombstone and bulldozed the cemetery! No one wrote to tell me. There I was, a bunch of flowers in my hand and she had disappeared! It is typical of the DDR. What a *scandal*!'

We left promptly after breakfast for Halle in his enormous Mercedes. The little East German Trabants and Wartburgs on the road made way for our great battleship of a car, which bounced and groaned as it sped along the dusty motorway. The old Dresdener opened the car windows wide. Frank Sinatra and a variety of Big Band sounds boomed from the cassette player. We passed a petrol station and the old Dresdener slapped his thigh.

'Just *look* at them! Poor as church mice. My God we have it good in Munich!'

He loved to talk about Churchill, to whose tomb in St Paul's cathedral he once made a special pilgrimage.

'There was a man one could respect. We need a Churchill in the Federal Republic. There is too little order around nowadays.'

I suggested that if 'order' was what he wanted, he could consider retiring in Dresden. There was plenty of order in the DDR. He found this suggestion most piquant.

He stopped the car and enquired about directions from a small crowd of people waiting by the roadside. Down purred the electric window. Out popped the shock of white hair. Above the Big Band sound booming in the background he shouted: 'Madam! Which way is it to Halle?'

I felt embarrassed by the noise of the music and the size of the automobile. I was sure his confident assumption of camaraderie would be rebuffed. I was wrong. The East Germans looked amused by his bombastic panache. Perhaps they recognised the broad Saxon accent of the smart lad from Dresden and admired the gall of one who had so brazenly got away.

WEIMAR

Art and science

GRACIOUS WEIMAR. No one could fail to be soothed by the autumnal glow of its pastel shades. What connotations are evoked by the name of Weimar, of Goethe, Schiller, Bach, Liszt and that kindly old Germany of the eighteenth century, when the fires of Luther's protest had mellowed into an enlightened and disinterested classicism. How curious that Weimar's name has most often been associated with that damp squib of a republic that lasted from 1919 to 1933.

All the tributaries of German culture seem to gather in a great confluence in the city of Weimar. The world of Wittenberg and Quedlinburg, the anxious and crabbed Germany of the high Middle Ages with all its religious and social tensions, vanishes like a night fever into Weimar's serene and smiling façades.

The sheer weight, the essential seriousness, of German culture in the age of the enlightenment descends onto the shoulders of the most casual visitor to Weimar. The city has no comparison in England. Weimar is too kindly a city to be a truly kindred spirit to the puritanical and acerbic flavour of Cambridge. There are echoes of Bath and Oxford in the classical bridges and the orange-rose stone. But in Weimar there is no hint of Oxford's clerical or monastic air. Weimar has always been Athenian in its dedication to the pursuit of science and culture.

Weimar is a walkable city. It lies along the banks of the river Ilm, but between the city and the river is a wide meadow. This is Weimar's green lung. Weimar is a place not for motor cars, but for long and thoughtful walks along the riverside, crossing the rustic bridges and pausing to contemplate the statue of Shakespeare and the various follies which were erected at regular intervals in the meadow. There is a snatch of a ruined abbey, a grotto and a Roman villa. Between them is a charming cottage, Goethe's 'garden house', where he lived upon first arriving in Weimar. Sheep still graze in the long grass of the meadow, watched over by shepherds and their dogs.

There is only one hotel for western visitors in Weimar, the delightful old 'Elephant'. In most cities in East Germany one is forced to stay in anonymous modern establishments which have been specially earmarked for western tourists so that they can be isolated from unnecessary contact with citizens of the DDR. In the spacious halls and bars of the 'Elephant', however, east meets west on equal terms. It was not long before I made the acquaintance of a former director of children's television in the DDR, who was enlightening a bewildered-looking Hungarian teenager with some nuggets from Weimar's history at the hotel bar.

The director was a member of that small but significant elite of non-communists who have 'made it' in the DDR, as he was evangelical by churchmanship and Christian Democrat by politics. He was stung to the quick by what he considered ignorant criticism of East German politics, for when he informed me that he had once directed television programmes which covered East German elections, I blithely remarked that such programmes could hardly have caused nail-biting tension among the viewers. 'You are completely wrong', he said with some passion. 'Elections in the DDR are very exciting.'

Many English conservatives would have sympathised with the television director over what he regarded as the subversive line being pursued by the contemporary generation of clergymen, who he felt had an obligation to be a little more supportive of the government.

'It's just opposition, opposition, opposition nowadays,' he said. 'This Easter I went to church in Berlin with my neighbours. As they were both members of the party, I appreciated the effort they made to accompany me. We heard a political sermon of the most humiliating kind. I was so embarrassed that I insisted we should all walk out.'

At the age of sixty-five he cherished a dream of visiting Paris. As he was a pensioner he was permitted to go, but his wife was still working and therefore unable to accompany him and he would not go without her. At the age of seventy he would be able to accomplish a dream that is within the grasp of most English fifteen-year-olds. The only positive remark I can make about this situation is that the East German television director and his wife will be amongst the most appreciative visitors Paris has ever received.

The eminence Weimar gained through the circle of englightened philosophers and artists who gathered here in the eighteenth century was quite out of proportion to its small size. Though the city was founded in about 1250, the city only became significant after the defeat of the protestant princes at the hands of the imperial army of Charles v at Mühlberg in 1547, when Wittenberg lost its position as a Saxon ducal residence. Wittenberg's loss was Weimar's gain, for the Saxon Elector, John Frederick, chose Weimar as his new residence. With him came Wittenberg's octogenarian artist, Lucas Cranach the Elder, who died in Weimar in 1553 and is buried in the church of St Peter and St Paul.

In the last years of his life, Lucas Cranach began work on a new alterpiece for the church of St Peter and St Paul that would match the great altarpiece of St Mary's in Wittenberg.

The parish church of Weimar is associated in Germany with the name of the eighteenth-century pastor, Herder, an associate of Goethe's and a member of the circle of enlightened thinkers who gathered around the Duchess Amelia in Weimar castle.

The church was built between 1245 and 1249 and rebuilt in its present late gothic style in 1500. Unlike so many churches in the DDR, St Peter and St Paul has a beautifully painted interior of vivid rococo pinks and blues, which forms a pleasant backdrop to the Cranach altarpiece. The altarpiece depicts Cranach's old colleage and intimate for forty years in Wittenberg, the reformer Martin Luther. In his company are John Frederick, the Elector of Saxony, to whom Cranach owed his new residence in Weimar, his wife Sybil of Cleves and their three sons. The elder Cranach had time only to draw up the plans for the alterpiece before he himself was buried in St Peter and St Paul. The execution of the painting therefore was left to his son, Cranach the Younger.

As the star of Wittenberg waned, the golden age of Weimar began. It was a new age for Germany as well, the age of the 'Enlightenment'. The arrival of this philosophical movement in Weimar is associated with the name of Anna Amelia, Duchess of Saxony-Weimar from 1756 until her death in 1807. The Wittumspalais, the former Franciscan monastery in which Luther had occasionally stayed, was the residence of the Duchess in the years of her retirement and is now a museum to the life and refined tastes of this remarkable eighteenth-century intellectual. A portrait of her in the Wittumspalais shows a highly intelligent, somewhat humorous woman.

Her married life was exceedingly short and her subsequent powers of patronage were considerable, hence her devotion to the promulgation of culture and the arts. She arrived in Weimar at the tender age of sixteen as the bride of the eighteen-year-old Duke Ernest August Constantine. The new duchess, the fifth child of the Duke and Duchess of Braunschweig, had a wretched childhood in which her principal solace had been the study of nature. Her arrival in Weimar was, as she herself described it, a liberating experience. 'In my sixteenth year I was released from my bondage,' she later commented. The duke died within two years of their marriage, leaving her with two children and the responsibility for governing the duchy. Although it was unusual for women to govern in these times, the nineteen-year-old duchess insisted on assuming the presidency over the council of the duchy in 1759.

The duchess was a great success, not only in reorganising the council's finances, but in opening libraries and theatres to the general public and presiding over salons to which the most eminent artists and *hommes de belles lettres* such as Wieland, Goethe, Herder and Schiller were invited to read translations of foreign authors, to discuss philosophy, poetry, art, or play music. Even the lesser lights in Duchess Amelia's circle contributed to the Weimar enlightenment, such as Frederick Bertuch, who founded the first German fashion magazine, the *Journal des Luxus und der Moden*, wrote several plays, and promoted the works of Cervantes. Some intellectual women were also associated with the cultural movement in Weimar, such as the actress and singer Corona Schröter, who was invited to Weimar from Leipzig by Goethe, Goethe's beloved Charlotte von Stein, and the duchess's lady in waiting, Lousie von Göchhausen. The flavour of the duchess's charmed evenings in Weimar castle was captured by an entry in the diary of Herder:

> At home with the Duchess, Monday was spent as usual. A few pieces from Shakespeare, Lessing's Nathan and Emilia, Goethe's Iphigenia, Tasso, Die Voegel, Wieland's Pervonte, Liebe und Liebe, Das Voegelchen, Der Zaun and others were delivered, very charmingly, and I must confess that Wieland's poems never appeared in so attractive a light.

Most importantly, the Duchess Amelia entrusted the education of the future duke, her son Carl August, to the learned translator of Shakespeare, Christopher Wieland, professor of philosophy in the university of Erfurt, so ensuring the continuity of her ideas in the Duchy of Weimar after her retirement. After seventeen years as regent, the Duchess Amelia retired to devote herself to her explorations of literature and science in the privacy of the Wittumspalais and handed over the reins of office to her son.

Amelia's son, the Duke Carl, proved himself worthy of his education by choosing Goethe as his minister and confidant. Goethe lived in the little 'garden house' by the river when he first arrived in Weimar but in 1782, as his position grew in importance in the counsels of the duke, he moved to a larger residence on the Frauenplan that is now a museum to the life of Germany's great philosopher.

High office did not dull the keenness of the chief minister's dedication to the pursuit of knowledge. On receiving his new quarters in the Frauenplan, Goethe told the duke in 1806 that he 'did not furnish the house for a life of pleasure but to propagate art and science if possible', and as if to corroborate this he informed another acquaintance that he believed 'sumptuous rooms and elegant furniture are for people who do not have thoughts ... as you know there is no sofa in my room: I like to sit on my old wooden chair ..., a surrounding of commodious furniture suspends my thinking.'

The house on the Frauenplan still contains the little bedroom overlooking the garden where he died, seated in an armchair, on 22 March 1832. In it he left some of the 18,000 minerals and 11,000 prints and drawings and 348 sculptures he had collected in his lifetime.

In his last will and testament he described his estate as 'important, not only for my descendants but for the whole of intellectual Weimar, yes indeed for all of Germany ... it is not likely to occur again that so much and so multifarious a possession will come together. I was exceptionally well favoured by fortune, the well-meaning of my contemporaries and my longevity. For sixty years now I have spent at least ten ducats a year for the purchase of curiosities. Much more was presented to me. It would be a pity if all this would be scattered about.' Goethe's hopes were only partially realised. The house was badly maintained after his death and one foreign visitor described the 'doleful and ruinous impression' it made on those who passed by.

The mausoleum dedicated to Goethe and Schiller was unveiled in 1857. It became the occasion of an official visit to Goethe's old house on the Frauenplan, which was conducted 'speedily and frigidly'. When the house devolved from Goethe's heirs to the Grand Duchy of Saxony-Weimar, the house on the Frauenplan was promptly opened as a museum in 1885.

The mausoleum itself adjoins, somewhat curiously, a Russian orthodox church, whose onion-shaped domes peep incongruously through the greenery of the park. The mausoleum is a ghoulish place, thoroughly imbued with a nineteenth-century obsession with making death as pompous as possible. The two coffins stand side by side, near the railed-off sarcophogi of various Grand Duchesses of Saxony-Weimar.

The Russian orthodox church behind the mausoleum, dedicated to St Mary Magdalen, is 'a little island of orthodoxy in a German sea', as one former pastor of St Mary Magdalen, the Archpriest Andrej Melnik, wrote. It has its own intriguing history.

The church was built by Duke Carl Alexander according to the will of his mother Maria Pavlovna, the daughter of Tsar Paul I, who died in 1859. The Grand Duchess Maria remained faithful to the orthodox religion of her mother country and only one month after her arrival in Weimar in 1804 she erected an orthodox chapel in the ducal castle. Her chaplain was a highly educated man, the Archpriest Nikita Jasnowskij, who translated the orthodox liturgy into German.

After Maria's death in 1859, work was begun on building an orthodox church near the ducal mausoleum. The foundation stone was laid on earth that was specially transported to Weimar from Russia. With the closure of the Russian legation in Weimar the church temporarily ceased to function, but owing to the kindly eye with which Stalin viewed the orthodox church in the last years of his life the church was reopened in 1950 and now belongs to the orthodox Exarchate of Central Europe.

The East Germans are great lovers of museum houses dedicated to the great names of German literature and culture and I lost count of the number of 'Lutherhouses', for example, which I visited in the DDR. The approbation with which these houses of culture are viewed by the authorities is no doubt influenced by the fact that those they commemorate are all safely dead and therefore unable to say anything nasty about the DDR. Cranach was ready and willing to serve a number of ideologically opposed patrons, but whether Goethe or the Duchess Amelia would have found the DDR a worthy successor to the Weimar enlightenment is something we will never know. It is enough that they have been appropriated as footsoldiers in the march of progress towards the year 1949.

The East German 'group tours' round these houses of culture have sometimes become the object of cheap jeers from British journalists, who find much ribald humour in the sight of the now-famous German *gruppen*, filing obediently round these establishments in crocodile formation. Why this should be so offensive is a mystery. The East German *gruppen* are one of the more charming sights in the DDR, as they move slowly and seriously round the 'Lutherstube' or the 'Goethehaus', heads reverently cocked on one side in concentration, as a teenage guide repeats a speech learnt by rote concerning this or that building's association with the rise of the bourgeoisie or the fall of feudalism. East Germany remains so rarely visited by tourists that even a town as densely clustered with the monuments of past greatness as Weimar appears almost deserted in comparison to cities of similar interest elsewhere in Europe.

At least the East Germans listen. The most irritating *gruppen* I came across were a party of English tourists noisily making their way round the 'Liszthaus' in Marienstrasse and who blocked out the entire speech of the guide by discussing what cakes they had eaten and whether the toilets functioned in the hotel.

'Of course, there's plenty to eat and that's the main thing,' said one middle-aged man as the guide discoursed about Liszt's career in Weimar.

'... and look at the children, so well behaved. It's nothing like in England, with all the vandalism,' answered his colleague.

The Liszthaus stands on the west side on the Ilm park. Here, in the house that formerly belonged to the court gardener, Franz Liszt lived from 1869 until his death in 1886. Liszt first settled in Weimar in 1848 in a house in the Altenburg district of the city which has since been destroyed.

After a life of wandering in Paris, Berlin, Hungary and Russia, and a tempestuous marriage with Countess Marie d'Agoult, Liszt had grown tired of a peripatetic existence, 'being paid as if I was a juggler' and moved to Weimar to take up his appointment as *Opernkappellmeister* in 1848. With him came the Countess Caroline von Sayn-Wittgenstein, who hastily separated from her husband, and her daughter, whom he had met in Kiev.

Europe was experiencing the 'springtime of revolutions' that was destroying the ordered classical world of Goethe. Liszt's sympathies were fully engaged with the revolutionaries in France and Hungary by whom he was inspired in the *Hungaria-kantate* and the *Héroïde Funèbre*. In a letter to the Countess Caroline on 24 March 1848 he wrote, 'my countrymen are in the act of taking such decisive, such Hungarian and such discouraged steps that it is impossible to deny them a tribute of true sympathy.'

The events of the 1848 revolution brought him close to Richard Wagner. As Wagner had taken part in the revolution in Dresden and had been subsequently expelled from the Duchy, Liszt was able to help him escape to Switzerland. Liszt was immediately struck by Wagner, writing in 1849 that 'Richard Wagner, *kapellmeister* from Dresden, has been here since yesterday. That is a man of admirable genius, such a head-splitting genius that he passes in this land for a new and shining phenomenon in art.' Wagner later married Liszt's daughter, Cosima. It was on a visit to his daughter Cosima Wagner in Bayreuth in the summer of 1886 that Liszt died, and there he was buried.

The name of Weimar in England is most often linked with the least glorious episode in the history of the city, namely the foundation of the doomed republic, which limped miserably along for fifteen years between 1918 and 1933 before being superceded by the ex-Viennese artist and Jew-baiter, Adolf Hitler. There is no museum in the DDR or in Weimar to the so-called 'Weimar Republic', which is rarely referred to in official literature.

In 1918 the unworthy son of our Princess Victoria, the Emperor William II, having declared that 'a descendant of Frederick the Great does not abdicate', promptly abdicated after hearing that the equally blue-blooded descendants of Peter the Great had been massacred at Ekaterinburg. He departed for an honourable retirement in Doorn, in Holland, where he fed ducks and was polite to everyone.

Germany was therefore, *ipso facto* of William's abdication rather than from any conscious desire, a republic. The politicians of the centre and the moderate left who were left anxiously holding the reins of power were appalled by the revolutionary temper of Berlin. They therefore chose Weimar as the venue of the first national constituent assembly. It was linked with the most progressive and democratic elements of German history. It was the city of Goethe and Schiller with a constitutional history untainted by Prussian militarism. The Grand Duchy had been granted a liberal constitution in 1817 in the days when Goethe was chief minister for the Duke Carl Alexander. It was also a very long way from Berlin and Rosa Luxemburg.

Elections were held on 19 January 1919. The Social Democrats, the largely catholic Centre party and the German Democratic party won the most votes and cobbled together a coalition. The Social Democratic leader Frederick Ebert was elected President of the Republic. Parliament was opened in Weimar's New National Theatre on 6 February 1919. The Weimar Republic began inauspiciously. President Ebert, ringed by tulips, was cat-called in his opening speech.

I left Weimar with a kind of dread. Without underestimating the real differences between life in East Germany and England in terms of freedom of movement and the rights of the individual against the prerogatives of the state, East Germany remained for me a familiar and confortable terrain. Forty years of domination by the Soviet Union had not erased a million tiny landmarks which subconsciously reassured me that I was still 'home'. The Wall in Berlin is a barrier only to those who are attempting to travel from the east to the west. For those like me who were travelling in the opposite direction from Berlin to Leningrad it was an irrelevancy, no more real than an advertisement informing me that the rest of Europe from here on lay in the orbit of a different superpower from the land whence I came. In all other respects, the land to the east of the Wall was more familiar to me than the west coast of America, and a great deal more familiar than, say, Japan, which was officially, by virtue of economic reasons, a part of 'the west'.

In England some people had envied my travelling to Czechoslovakia. Czechoslovakia had had its 'Prague Spring' and that nice Mr Dubcek. As my train rumbled through Dresden and on to the Czech frontier I felt wholly uncommiserated by the knowledge that the Czechs were thirsting for parliamentary democracy. It was a poor compensation for not being able to understand what people were saying in their own tongue. We approached the Czech frontier. Miserably I handed over my passport. Once again I was crossing over the Wall.

PRAGUE

Arrival

THERE WERE policemen in the Wenceslas Square in the centre of Prague. The city was bracing itself for the twentieth anniversary of the 'Prague Spring', when Mr Dubcek had vainly attempted to graft a little of the traditions of Czechoslovakia's pre-war democracy on to the regime that had been power since the February revolution of 1948.

I scurried through the streets trying to look inoffensive, clutching a voucher issued by the Czechoslovak tourist office in London. It claimed to entitle me to say in the house of a Czech family in the Prague suburb of Budejevicka for a week and a half.

My hosts looked surprised when I turned up outside their swanky new villa with a shiny new Skoda in the porch, pulling my black suitcase on wheels behind me. They were sunbathing in the garden with scarcely any clothes on, a lean and handsome couple in their forties with lupine smiles. The woman examined my voucher.

'This is a problem,' she said. 'I have already let out the room to a couple from Hungary.'

My face fell. The Czech tourist authority had obviously bungled. I felt like saying 'This could never happen in the DDR', but checked myself when I remembered that it was much more difficult to stay in private homes in the DDR in the first place. The handsome couple looked sympathetic.

'You can stay here if you are tired,' said the wife. She went inside

74

to confer with her husband whilst I waited uneasily on the porch. From inside I heard the sound of raised voices, a man shouting, then absolute silence. The woman re-emerged with a taught smile.

'Yes, it's fine,' she said, 'you can sleep in our bedroom. My husband and I will sleep on the couch downstairs.'

That evening my hostess and I played word-games in the kitchen. I would mention a famous Czechoslovak politician and she would shout out whether they were Czech or Slovak.

'Masaryk?'

'Czech!'

'Gottwald?'

'Also Czech!'

'Gustav Husak?'

'Slovak!'

'Alexander Dubcek?'

'... also Slovak.' She disappeared hurriedly to fetch some more beers. The game was over. It was difficult to tell who had won as I had so obviously spoilt everything. Unfortunately I had simply run out of politicians.

She spoke little English, which invested her conversation with a peculiar poignancy and directness. 'I am a grandmother,' she said, pouring me another lager with eyes that pleaded for me to refute this statement.

'I don't believe it.' I obliged cheerfully.

'Yes, I play much sport. Swimming. Weights. I stay young. But my husband ... he is old.' After hearing that, I put on that bland smile I had been taught in the seminary for dealing with difficult parishioners.

'Please, come this way.' She got up and beckoned me into the living room.

'Weights,' she said, opening a large drawer in the cupboard. She pulled out a large bell from the drawer.

'Watch me,' she said as she began to flex her considerable muscles, lifting the weights up and down, one two, one two.

The following morning I telephoned the Czech tourist authority in Prague and asked them where I was staying.

'You are in Leninova,' said a woman on the other end of the line.

'Ah, but I'm not. I am in Budejovicka,' I replied.

There was a short silence.

'Why are you in Budejovicka?'

'Because that is the address of the voucher I received in London.'

'Then you are in the wrong address. Please come to our office immediately and go to a new address in Leninova.'

I arrived at the Czech tourist office, bewildered by the sound of familiar English and American voices around me. The bureau resembled one of those refugee centres set up by the Allies in Berlin after the end of the Second World War. There was a row of glass-fronted booths behind which sat another row of harassed-looking tourist officials. Around them, a throng of desperate, frightened tourists swarmed like angry bees. Someone was crying, someone else was shouting, and too many phones were ringing. The weeping came from an elderly American lady in her seventies.

'Why won't you help me?' she said between chokes. 'Why won't you just *help* me?'

'Because you are in the wrong queue,' hissed the Czech official, her eyes narrowing. 'You must go to booth number three.'

The American lady took one look at the column of people camping outside booth number three and choked again. It was interesting how the desperate situation had stripped away the veneer of humanity with which most civilised people conduct their daily lives. In any normal course of events, most of the people in the tourist bureau would have gone out of their way to help this elderly foreigner. The strain of a morning spent arguing with Czech officialdom, however, had reduced even the most sensitive spirits to savagery. There was a callous and audible sigh of relief from the mob behind the old lady from America when she finally tottered out of the door having uttered one last 'help'. We surged gratefully forward, jostling and shoving.

My new home was in a very different district from Budejovicka. Leninova was as proletarian as its name suggested, consisting of a cluster of bald and rickety-looking tower-blocks on a hill above the city. A pungent lift transported me to the sixth floor.

I knocked on the door, which was opened by a sulky blonde of about twenty. Behind her I glanced into a bare, bookless flat which was enveloped in a thick fog of cigarette smoke.

'Where were you last night?' she opened. Before I had time to answer, she said, 'Well it doesn't matter anyhow. Shut the door. You are letting in the wind.'

'Oh, I am sorry. Do you prefer to speak in English or German because I do not speak Cz . . .'

'Why do you think I speak German? This is Czechoslovakia.'

'I just . . .

'Here is your room. Don't ever forget to shut the window *and* the door when you go out. You will let in the wind. You haven't said where you were last night.'

'Well, the train was late from Dresden and . . .'

'That's normal in socialist countries. Never mind. Are you going into Prague?'

'I thought I might.'

'There is a tram. Do you have tickets?'

'No.'

'That's a pity. You will have to walk.'

PRAGUE

Old Town

'It is as a green garden to our eyes and the personal
delight of Our Majesty.'

Charles IV, King of Bohemia, on the city of Prague

MY EYES FEASTED on the paintwork in Prague. The city has been
immaculately restored in a manner that puts the East Germans to
shame. After Berlin, Prague gleamed. Prague is a rich city, not merely
in relics of the Habsburg empire, but in a contemporary prosperity.
The Czech economy is creaking a little nowadays, but it does not
show in the cafés stocked with Viennese-style torten, in the warm
and beery taverns or in the streets of the middle-class suburbs.

Prague is dominated by the magnificence of its churches, which
alone gives the city an entirely different flavour from that of Berlin.
Berlin is a secular city. It reflects the fluid and adaptable character
of the Prussians. The mawkish sentimentality they display in fits and
spasms towards the relics of the medieval past complements their
brisk determination to make the best of things as they are. For Berlin
has been spun around the dance floor fast and often by a great many
partners. The results are Berlin's dizziness, its practicality, a tendency
to publicly bend whichever way the wind is blowing, superficial
enthusiasms and an abiding optimism that everything will be all right
in the end.

Prague is as righteous as Berlin is flexible. Its character is that
of a disappointed idealist. The important passages in the history of

Prague have involved embracing somewhat hopeless religious or in modern times 'idealistic' causes that would leave most Prussians cold. It is as inflexible as Berlin is adaptable. So Prague is rooted irrevocably in the past, from which, however, it derives no consolation. Like the Bourbons it has forgotten nothing and learnt nothing. It is a city which has neither forgotten its past triumphs nor forgiven its recent calamities. Behind the gleaming paintwork and the robe of baroque churches, Prague is a sadder, more disappointed city than Berlin.

The results are the people of Prague's fundamental pessimism and their tendency to search continually for someone to blame for their present misfortunes. The Berliners blame neither the Russians for occupying them or the English for razing their city to the ground. The Praguers never cease to rail against the Russians for occupying them and the English for betraying them at Munich in 1938.

There is a magnificent bridge named after Prague's most munificent patron, Charles IV, King of Bohemia and Holy Roman Emperor; a rather bland castle; some renaissance noblemen's palaces and a marvellous clock in the town hall square. They are overshadowed by the floating domes of vast baroque churches and the fanciful cupolas of convents.

The cathedral of St Vitus squats like a black raven in its eyrie over the red roofs and ochre spires that tumble down the hill towards the banks of the river Vltava. Behind the cathedral lies the bejewelled baroque shrine of the Prague Loretto. At the bottom of the hill, the Charles Bridge which links the New Town to the Old Town is lined with the statues of saints and apostles of Bohemia. On the other side of the river in the old town square stands the best known church of all, the Tyn church.

The impression of a great catholic city is deceptive. The architecture of Prague is the architecture of conquest and alien domination. The catholicism professed rather ambivalently by most Czechs today is that of a religion imposed by the swords of the catholic armies of the Habsburg emperors which subdued Bohemia in 1620.

That Prague would later become the provincial capital of a subject nation under the domination of Austria would have seemed incredible two centuries previously. The Czechs have always been Europe's 'enemies of promise'.

The medieval kingdom of Bohemia had all the makings of a great nation state along the lines of France, England or Castille. The Premyslid dynasty in the twelfth and thirteenth centuries laid the foundations of a strong royal government which might in time have enabled the kings of Bohemia to tame the feudal lords as the Tudors tamed them in England. Complementing the formation of a strong royal government in Bohemia was the establishment of a unified Bohemian church. In the late fourteenth century the newly established Archbishopric of Prague was released from its dependency on the See of Mainz.

The land of Bohemia was fecund, dotted with silver mines and capable of producing great wealth. In fourteenth-century Prague, Bohemia possessed a great capital of some 60,000 people, a cosmopolitan and enquiring citizenry of Czechs and Germans. There was a large Jewish community that led to the city being called 'the Jerusalem of Europe'. Most importantly of all, fourteenth-century Prague possessed the only university in the Holy Roman Empire, indeed the only university in all of central and eastern Europe, the celebrated Charles University.

In 1348, Charles IV, King of Bohemia and future Holy Roman Emperor, issued the Golden Bull for the foundation of a university in Prague: 'For our heartfelt love of our hereditary kingdom of Bohemia impells us to exalt it more generously by especial titles of privilege, for it is as a green garden to our eyes and the personal delight of Our Majesty.'

The university was organised into four 'nations', whose voting rights controlled the government of the university. Three of these 'nations', the Bavarian, Saxon and Polish, were dominated by Germans. There was nothing unusual in this. Charles intended the university to serve the interests of the Holy Roman Empire as a whole and Prague was a multinational city of German and Czech Bohemians. The Germans had been in Prague since the tenth century and their numbers increased in the twelfth century when the Premyslid Dukes of Bohemia offered German immigrants certain privileges and immunities if they would settle in the city. The German merchants of the Old Town were the cultural and economic superiors of the Czech peasants and artisans in the New Town and naturally enough, in the first decades of the life of the university, they supplied the overwhelming majority of the academic staff. But in the 'green garden' of Bohemia, towards the end of the fourteenth century, the Czech Cains had begun to conceive of a great jealously towards the more highly favoured German Abels.

The intellectual leaders among the Czechs expressed their hostility to the Germans through an idealistic movement for religious reform. They found their spokesman in an adventurous clergyman by the name of Jan Huss.

The fourteenth-century Tyn church beside the Old Town square is where the movement for the reformation of the church in Prague and Bohemia began. The interior of the church today is like that of any baroque catholic church and is cluttered with moribund relics of the faith of the counter-reformation. In the 1360s, when it was built, it was a lighter, sparer place whose congregations thrilled to the fiery sermons of a hot-gospelling Austrian friar by the name of Konrad Waldhauser. Waldhauser was an Austrian and the congregations he excited with his denunciations of clerical avarice and corruption were the German merchants of the Old Town. We may imagine the bowed heads of the three German burghers as they piously absorbed the preacher's earnest injunctions for spiritual reform in Bohemia. In and amongst the Germans burghers, however, we may also imagine a few Czech Bohemians. For it was on the fertile soil of Czech jealousy that Konrad Waldhauser's words had the most lasting impact.

Not far from the Tyn church is the Bethlehem chapel, which witnessed the second stage of the Czech reformation. In the Bethlehem chapel one feels closer to the spirit of the fourteenth-century Czech reformers. The church was almost entirely demolished in the eighteenth century and has been recently rebuilt in a style that would have been more familiar to the Praguers of the fourteenth century. It is a cool and spacious hall with no other furniture than a pulpit. Biblical texts are the only adornment on the walls.

The Bethlehem chapel was built in 1391 at the subscription of Czech courtiers of King Wenceslas, the son of Charles IV. Its erection was a turning point in the history of Prague, because the Bethlehem chapel was founded as a church where the services were held only in the Czech language rather than in German, the language of the old 'ascendancy'. The building of the Bethlehem was a symbol of the growing assertiveness of the Czech population in Prague, and it coincided in time with the increasingly bitter struggle for power between the Czech and German fellows over the control of the Charles University. The Bethlehem chapel soon assumed the reforming mantle of Waldhauser in the Tyn church, for its services were orientated around fiery biblical expositions by the leading Czech preachers. From 1402 the incumbent was Jan Huss.

Jan Huss, whose statue dominates the Old Town square, was born in 1369, in the village of Husinec on the frontier between Bohemia and Bavaria. Here the two-century-old ascendancy of the Teutonic race rubbed abrasively against the suppressed ambitions of the Slavs. To Huss, therefore, the friction between Germans and Czechs in the Charles University was not merely an academic dispute over philosophy or even over the finer points of Christian dogma. Ethnic rivalry was as natural to him as his mother's milk.

By the time that Jan Huss became rector of the Charles University, in 1402, the theological disputes between Germans and Czechs had so sharpened as to raise suspicions among the Germans that their opponents were rank heretics.

The books of the Oxford don and heretic John Wycliffe were seeping into the Charles University and spreading ideas of a more biblically orientated religion, which would be propagated by services in the vernacular tongue rather than Latin and which would be organised into an independent national church under royal rather than papal suzerainty.

In his home country, Wycliffe was never much more than a fly in the ecclesiastical ointment. Wycliffe was a peevish and disappointed Oxford don, whose enthusiastic support for royal power over the church, coupled with calls for the disendowment of monasteries, led to his being briefly championed by anti-clerical circles at court. He was a useful weapon with which to frighten the ecclesiastical authorities in Rome.

When Wycliffe's aristocratic patrons read the finer print of his writings, however, they became nervous. Wycliffe had based his opposition to the pretensions of the clergy on a curious belief culled from the musings of an Irish prelate, Archbishop Fitzralph of Armagh, known as 'Dominion by Grace'. This suggested that ecclesiastical power was only legitimately exercised by those in a state of spiritual grace.

To suggest that an illiterate parish priest who had been fiddling with the baker's wife was unable to celebrate an efficacious sacrament was one thing. But if 'Dominion by Grace' was extended to the sphere of secular government, the implications were little short of revolutionary. What would happen if some bold spirits applied 'Dominion by Grace' to the prerogatives of the king, or to the hereditary privileges of the great lords themselves ...?

Wycliffe was hurriedly exiled to the obscure rectory of Lutterworth, though not before his ideas had spawned an anti-clerical sect among the artisans of the towns. The leaders of church and state, however, allied to prosecute and burn as many of Wycliffe's followers as they apprehended.

The German professors at the Charles University in Prague were every bit as suspicious of Wycliffe as the English bishops. The more they called for the burning of Wycliffe's books, however, the more the radical Czech reformers gathered around Jan Huss rallied in Wycliffe's defence. The Germans carried the day. With the approval of Archbishop Zybnek, Wycliffe's books were ceremonially burnt in 1403.

The burning of Wycliffe's books was the last victory of the German 'nations' in the Charles University. King Wenceslas and Queen Zofie had noted the fratricidal struggle between Germans and Czechs in the university with interest. They decided to side with the latter. The queen was moved by Huss's evangelical fervour. The king had decided that the German minority was as an unreliable force and must therefore be expelled. President Beneš reached the same decision with regard to the Sudetenland Germans after the Second World War.

In 1409, King Wenceslas took a momentous decision for the future of Bohemia. The king published the Decree of Kutna Hora, abolishing in a stroke the voting rights of the Bavarian, Saxon and Polish nations in the university. The decree stated that: 'the German nation ... has in all the business of the university arrogated to itself the use of three votes, while the Bohemian nation ... has and uses only one. The king commands ... the rector and the university that hereafter the Bohemian nation ... shall enjoy the right to three votes.'

In a single stroke Wenceslas had turned the Golden Bull of his father on its head. The work of his father in establishing the Charles University as an international university for a multinational kingdom like Bohemia was undone. Instead the university was to be an instrument of Czech supremacy. The German fellows emigrated *en masse* for the new university of Leipzig, carrying bitter memories with them in their baggage. Jan Huss had triumphed over the historic Teutonic enemy.

The disaster that was to bring ruin to the 'green garden' of Charles IV, that was to reduce the Charles University to a provincial institution, that was to turn the great crown of Bohemia into the booby prize of Europe to be passed around the indigent princelings of Germany, was unravelling.

The events in Bohemia outraged Christendom. For after the triumph at Kutna Hora, the Czech reformers began boldly to flout the authority of the pope and the Archbishop of Prague. The German merchants were attacked in Prague. Monasteries were siezed. The Czech clergy began to administer the chalice to the laity in Holy Communion, in defiance of Catholic dogma. Huss himself had been excommunicated in 1410 and the entire city of Prague placed under an interdict since 1412. The sinners not only remained impenitent. They appeared to revel in righteous, but suicidal, opposition to the *force majeure* of pope and emperor.

A council of the catholic church took place at Constance, much to the displeasure of the pope who preferred to manage the affairs of the church unaided. Both pope and council were keen to assert their unimpeachable orthodoxy by the prosecution of heresy. Bohemia therefore figured high on everyone's agenda.

Jan Huss was summoned to Constance to answer the charges levelled against him in 1414 and, knowingly, he took the road to Golgotha. Like Luther at the Diet of Worms, Huss was promised the royal protection of King Wenceslas's brother King Sigismund of Hungary. But Huss was not as secure in the affections of Sigismund as was Luther in those of the Elector of Saxony. Huss was betrayed. On July 1415 he was stripped of his vestments and heard the dreadful words that were spoken over the heads of heretics: 'We commend your spirit to the devil.' He was burnt to death outside the city of Constance on the same day.

The burning of Huss threw Bohemia into revolt. After the death of King Wenceslas, the Bohemians refused to accept his brother and heir, King Sigismund, as King of Bohemia. The king's catholic councillors were thrown out of the town hall windows. This was the first 'defenestration of Prague'.

The See of Prague lay vacant, its patrimony despoiled. Time and time again the rebel armies of Bohemia defeated the papal and imperial armies sent against them and from 1471 the catholic kings of Bohemia were forced to accept the existence of an independent national church based on the teachings of Huss.

The price of this dubious asset was enormous. Incessant wars devastated the towns. Royal power disintegrated to such an extent that the crown of Bohemia became a worthless bauble no self-respecting prince would accept. The monasteries were plundered by the great lords who exercised greater and greater influence over the government of the kingdom. A once free peasantry slid inexorably into serfdom.

The town hall stands opposite the Tyn church in Old Town square. Now it is half-ruined, one of the few irreperable casualties of the Nazi occupation. On the hour, every hour, a large crowd of tourists gather in the square to watch the Twelve Apostles emerge from the fifteenth-century clock on the town hall wall.

The town hall was the scene of the last chapter in Bohemia's vain attempt to hold on to the independence that was gained at such a prohibitive cost after the burning of Jan Huss at Constance.

In 1618, the Holy Roman Emperor led an assault on the privileges of Bohemia's protestant lords. Once again, the Czech protestants replied by hurling the emperor's catholic regents out of the town hall window. It was the second 'defenstration of Prague'.

The rebels deposed the emperor and elected as their king an obscure protestant prince, Frederick v of the Palatinate. His wife was an English princess, Elizabeth Stuart, the daughter of James I. A romantic legend has grown up around the persons of the 'Winter King' and his English 'Winter Queen', for no particular reason other than the brevity of their rule. Frederick was infamous during his short stay in Prague for the particular cruelty of his dealings with the peasants and serfs. The Winter Queen's most celebrated act was to order the ancient crucifix on the Charles Bridge to be hurled into the waters of the Vltava. Between the two of them they destroyed a great many religious images, but did not, however, win any battles. There was no repeat of the great Hussite victories nearly two centuries earlier. The patrimony of Charles IV's 'green garden' was exhausted. The impoverished and enserfed peasants did not rise in defence of their unknown prince or the Czech protestant lords, to whom they had no cause whatsoever to be grateful. The imperial army routed Frederick's forces within less than an hour at the White Mountain outside Prague on 8 November 1620. The Winter King and Winter Queen scuttled out of Prague the same evening. The era of Huss and of Bohemian independence went out, not with a bang but a whimper.

The modern face of Prague, of statues of St Nepomuk, of wayside crucifixes, of sculpted mitred bishops waving their episcopal staffs from the niches of baroque churches, was as alien to the Czechs as the construction of Stalin's Palace of Culture in post-war Warsaw. The Praguers came to love the buildings themselves, but they have never been more than lukewarm adherents to the Catholic creed these structures celebrated.

The sumptuous baroque shrine of the Prague Loretto lies behind the Hradcany castle. The moving spirit behind the Prague Loretto, which became the most splendid shrine in Bohemia, was a wealthy Czech countess, Benigna Katerina of Lobkovice, who had seen another Loretto shrine on her travels in Moravia.

The Loretto cult told of the miraculous transfer of the *santa casa*, in which the Archangel Gabriel had announced the birth of Christ to the Virgin Mary, to the Italian town of Loretto.

The legend began in the thirteenth century and was much favoured by the propagandists of the counter-reformation. So the construction of an imitation Loretto in Prague in 1626, only six years after the battle of the White Mountain, was a symbol of the new Austrian and Catholic supremacy over Bohemia.

The treasury of this gilded shrine was stuffed with diamond monstrances and golden relics that must have disgusted the religious sensibilities of the Czech protestants of Prague. The treasury was rebuilt twice in the course of the seventeenth century to accommodate the flow of donations from the families who had 'done well' out of 1620. To add insult to injury, the chapel of the Santa Casa in the central courtyard of the shrine was embellished with the arms of Tilly, the victorious general at the battle of the White Mountain.

The façade of the Loretto was not completed until the eighteenth century. It was the work of the family of Dientzenhofer, father and son, the architects of the largest baroque church in Prague, St Nicholas in the Lesser Quarter. Between them they made so great an impact on the face of Prague that the style of many of Prague's churches is often called 'Dientzenhofer baroque'.

The Santa Casa is enclosed by two-storey galleries. These contain chapels dedicated to various Spanish and Italian saints who had been the instruments of various bizarre and even ridiculous miracles. These the Austrian Jesuits now impressed on the recalcitrant citizenry of Prague as worthier subjects of veneration than Jan Huss.

One such chapel, for example, dating from the 1730s, contains a figure of a woman whose face is covered in hair. It represents St Starosta of Spain. According to legend, St Starosta, who is also known as St Vigilfortis, was ordered by her father to marry a pagan. Starosta prayed to be released from this dreadful fate and was answered in a most unusual manner. She grew a beard overnight. Whether St Starosta was grateful for being released from her obligation in so embarassing a manner is unknown. To a people accustomed to Jan Huss's earthenware gospel, it must have been very confusing. According to my guidebook, 'the cult of St Starosta had an alien effect on the Czech milieu and did not particularly spread throughout Bohemia.'

The counter-reformation in Prague did have a more charming and accessible side. Nestling beneath the Hradcany in Karmelitska is the church of Our Lady of Victories, which contains a small statue known as 'The Infant of Prague'.

The Infant was brought to Prague by a Spanish noblewoman whose daughter bequeathed the statue to the monastery of the Bare-foot Carmelites in 1628. The Infant became and remains the object of considerable veneration way beyond the borders of Bohemia. In the church porch a notice reads as follows:

The Carmelite fathers are still dreaming their eternal dream in
the quietness of the crypt beneath the High Altar and above
them the Holy Infant is still dealing out its benediction with
its small hand and welcoming with its charming smile all who
come and visit it.

PRAGUE

Revolutionaries

IN AUGUST 1875, a young Czech wrote a small autobiography describing his youth. In it he related how he 'saved myself from the moral corruption which affected my school fellows', and how when, years later, 'I found myself in the company of depraved students ... I thank God that he saved my moral purity. A certain modesty restrained me from the excesses which were then and there, the rule with young people.'

The young man left Prague for Vienna. 'Bookshops,' he remembered, 'were my only joy. I studied Atlases to find the page with my own country on it. Tears interrupted my pastime and night after night I cried myself to sleep.'

Four years after writing his biography, he completed a thesis on 'Suicide as a mass social phenomenon', in which he concluded that taking one's own life was 'the mathematical measure of the true mood of society'. The author of these fastidious, melancholy and self-righteous words was Thomas G, Masaryk, the first president of the independent state of Czechoslovakia.

Thomas Masaryk, like Gladstone!, was that remarkable phenomenon, the elderly revolutionary. Most of his working life revolved around the Philosophy Department of the University of Prague. But in his sixties, when most of his contemporaries were either dead or had achieved the serenity of old age, Masaryk became vociferously anti-Austrian. He told the guests at his sixtieth birthday party that they should 'put a stick of dynamite under Austria and blow it up. It deserves nothing else.'

At the still more advanced age of sixty-eight, Masaryk achieved his aim. Throughout the late nineteenth century the Czechs in Bohemia rediscovered the confidence that had been lost at the White Mountain in 1620. In the 1850s, the Czechs gained control for the first time over the municipality of Prague. Czech youths became keen adherents of sports clubs, which performed an ideological role of asserting the virility of the Czechs over the dominant Germans.

The strain of the First World War was too much for the old empire. The Emperor Karl, a winsome liberal in his thirties, was preparing a 'people's manifesto' which would guarantee full autonomy for all the nations of Austria-Hungary within a loose confederation.

The old philosophy professor of Prague was not going to be put off by that. In Washington, President Wilson, the fastidious former Princeton don, was examining the untidy borders of Europe with distaste. There was much rearranging to be done. He was visited by Masaryk, who now entertained dreams of a great Slavic confederation stretching from Prague to Moscow. Masaryk left disappointed, when Wilson declared himself unable to sanction the destruction of the Austro-Hungarian Empire.

In the summer of 1918 Masaryk's close colleague sent joyful news. France had recognised the Czech national council as the provisional government of the lands inhabited by the Czechs and the Slovaks. The French had told Beneš, 'We want to destroy Austria.'

Masaryk returned to Prague in triumph as the first President of Czechoslovakia. He declined the offer of a ceremonial entry into the city by carriage for one in a motor car.

There is no statue Thomas Masaryk in Prague. After the communist revolution of 1948 his memory was publicly effaced with the same thoroughness with which the Jesuits effaced the memory of Jan Huss after 1620.

Masaryk's monuments in Prague are the sleek Skoda cars of the 1930s that one can still see in the museum of industrial design and the strikingly forward-looking constructivist buildings erected in the Prague of the 1920s, such as the former Bata shoe shop in Wenceslas

Square, whose glass façade was a contemporary sensation.

Masaryk was, of course, not directly concerned with the design of Skoda cars or the erection of shoe shops, but nothing else illustrates more dazzlingly the optimism of the early days of the Czechoslovak republic, when Thomas Masaryk arrived in Prague not in a carriage but in the back seat of an automobile.

The Prague bourgeoisie took to architectural modernism with much more enthusiasm than did their German or English counterparts, for whom the Bauhaus school in Dessau remained exotic and distrusted.

In the late nineteenth century the streets of Prague had become a riot of competing styles emanating from Vienna. Art deco jostled with art nouveau. The fruits of this were immense art nouveau cafés, the Europa on Wenceslas Square, and the Obecni Dum on Republic Square, whose fey mosaics and gold-leaf balconies made the interior resemble the ballroom of a Cunard liner.

Some Czech architects favoured the creation of an imaginary 'Slavic' national architecture of the kind that was much favoured by the Serbians. The statue of King Wenceslas in Wenceslas Square, which was erected in 1915, was one of the finer pieces of this nostalgic and rather xenophobic architectual style.

After the proclamation of Czechoslovak independence, these styles became instantly discredited. The modernist mood of Prague in the 1920s and 1930s was an expression of the Czechs' confident internationalism and their rejection of the Habsburg past.

A world away from the sunny enthusiasm of the House of Bata is the Klement Gottwald museum. It commemorates the man whose spirit dominated the second quarter century of independent Czechoslovak history as much as Masaryk's spirit dominated the first.

There is no museum to Ulbricht in East Germany. The Hungarians would never tolerate any reminder of the terrible days of their first post-war communist premier, Rakosi. Nor would the authorities be so unwise as to attempt to erect one. There is a museum to Stalin in the Soviet Union, but it is tucked away in the obscure Georgian town where he was born. The Czechs, however, still maintain a museum dedicated to the Stalinist drone who plunged Czechoslovakia back into a new dark age.

The museum of Klement Gottwald is housed in a musty sarcophagus that used to be a savings bank. I found it quite empty except for a single attendant silently chewing bon-bons in one of the exhibition rooms.

In the entrance hall there is a statue of 'a worker' embracing 'a soldier' with such force that they appear to be French-kissing, though this effect was surely unintended. Above them is a ceiling decorated with a frieze of dumpy peasants. The exhibition includes a number of posters from the year 1948, the 'year Zero' of the new Czechoslovakia. One depicts a fat old woman waving one stout fist in the air and shouting 'volte communisty'. How many votes her fat and foolish face won for Gottwald's communists is a matter for speculation.

The Klement Gottwald museum does not enlighten the visitor much about the events of 1968, when Alexander Dubcek attempted to sweeten Gottwald's prison camp with a few of Thomas Masaryk's democratic principles. The Klement Gottwald museum describes the events of 1968 as follows:

> The emergence of revisionist and anti-socialist forces created conditions for the international assistance of fraternal socialist countries for the defence of socialism in Czechoslovakia and for overcoming the crisis by political means.

From the open glass façades of the House of Bata it is a long way to the dreary portals of the Klement Gottwald museum. The Czechs truly are the 'enemies of promise', forever snatching defeat from the jaws of victory. How did Charles IV's 'green garden', which had everything in the 1930s, become the country which had nothing in the 1950s? For a silence has descended on Czechoslovakia since 1948 much as a silence descended on Bohemia in 1620.

As has happened so often in Bohemian history, the fratricidal struggles between Czechs and Germans destroyed the harmony of Bohemia. For that, Thomas Masaryk bears a great deal of responsibility. Behind his democratic principles lay a determination as strong as Jan Huss's to assert the superiority of Czech Bohemian over German Bohemian. Masaryk spoke the language of President Wilson's 'fourteen points' by which national frontiers were to be determined on the basis of nationality, but he never conceded the same principle to the German Bohemians of the so-called 'Sudetenland', which bordered on Germany and Austria. Like the Hussites in the fifteenth century, he struck whilst the iron was hot and insisted on the creation of Czechoslovakia 'on maximum lines'.

The German Bohemians who were stranded inside the new state of Czechoslovakia after the Versailles Treaty of 1919 as a result of Masaryk's determination, and who made up a quarter of the adult population of the new state, were deeply unhappy with their enforced citizenship of Czechoslovakia. The Germans retained their schools, a university and a theatre in Prague which became a refuge for anti-Nazi German intellectuals fleeing Hitler's tyranny after 1933. The mass of German Bohemians were not, however, anti-Nazi intellectuals, but shopkeepers and farmers who were only too well aware that in 1918 they had been 'bounced' into an alien state against their express wishes.

Lord Runciman was sent on a mission by the British government to assess the validity of German claims to the Sudetenland before the Munich conference in 1938. He made the rather obvious point that German claims to German-speaking areas of Bohemia were largely justified. This was subsequently portrayed as a gross act of 'betrayal' by the British of a small nation that was standing up to Hitler. This, however, is retrospective thinking in the light of the subsequent war. Britain and Germany were not at war in 1938 and the Czechs were asking the British Prime Minister to initiate a war with Germany in order to defend their supremacy over a people who had never recognised the legitimacy of their claim to German-speaking Bohemia.

The outbreak of war between Germany and the Allies gave Masaryk's successor, Eduard Beneš, a historic opportunity to enact an irrevocable revenge on the luckless Germans of Bohemia. On the same grounds chosen by King Wenceslas in the decree of Kutna Hora, that the German minority formed a treasonous fifth column in Czechoslovakia, President Beneš declared that in the event of an Allied victory, the entire German population of Czechoslovakia, one in four of the population, would be expelled.

There was an Allied victory and the Germans were indeed expelled amid scenes of great brutality. The expulsion of the twenty-five thousand Germans from Bruenn, or Brno as it is now called, was recorded in a despatch by Rhona Churchill of the *Daily Mail*:

Shortly before 9 p.m. they marched through the streets calling
on all German citizens to be standing outside their front doors
at 9 o'clock with one piece of hand luggage each, ready to leave
the town forever. Then they were marched out of the town
at gunpoint, twenty-five thousand men, women and children.

The removal of this huge segment of the population of
Czechoslovakia upset the balance of Masaryk's democracy. Pre-war
Czechoslovakia possessed one of the largest communist parties in
Europe. It was led by the bilious Stalinist, Klement Gottwald.
Gottwald cannot be accused of having dissembled about his intentions
before the voters. In 1931 he told the members of the Czech national
assembly: 'real peace will only be achieved when you are hanging
from the lamp-posts.'

The expulsion of the Germans left the liberal political heirs of
Masaryk perilously exposed to Gottwald's communists, by whom
they were rapidly overwhelmed. There were vast communist demonstrations in Prague throughout 1947 and 1948. In the first free elections
after the war, Gottwald won an overwhelming endorsement from
the electorate. It was an extraordinary demonstration of national
boorishness. No other nation in Europe has handed itself over so
willingly to its executioner. Even with the aid of the Gestapo Hitler
had not managed to secure such a popular mandate. It is as if Clement
Attlee had won the British general election in 1945 on a manifesto
to imprison artists, abolish parliamentary democracy, execute his
political opponents and chain the country to Stalin's ankles.

History in Bohemia has always moved in circles rather than in
a straight line. Like the Bourbons, the Czechs neither learn nor forget
anything. Time and time again events repeat the past in uncanny
similitude.

Soon after Klement Gottwald's assumption of power in 1948, Jan
Masaryk, the last non-communist member in the government and
the son of the man who had called suicide 'the expression of the
mood of the nation', fell to his death from the window of the Foreign
Office. It was the third 'defenestration of Prague'.

PRAGUE

Jews

THE SECOND WORLD WAR took out two historic communities in Bohemia, Germans and Jews. The Germans disappeared on cattle trucks to Berlin. The Jews perished in camps and ovens. In the heart of the Old Town, near the banks of the river Vltana is a cluster of synagogues which once formed the core of the great Jewish ghetto of Prague. Here the Jews lived and maintained their own synagogues, cemeteries and a town hall from the time of the Third Lateran Council, which decided that Jews must live separately from Christians, until the ghetto was abolished by the Empress Maria Theresa.

It is a good place to begin a tour of the city as the Jewish community in Prague formed a remarkably stable element in the life of the city until the Nazi invasion, calmly going about its business whilst Germans and Czechs, catholics and protestants distracted Europe with their mutual massacres.

The Old New synagogue was built in the thirteenth century, when it was named the 'new' synagogue. By the sixteenth century, however, it had become, confusingly, the 'Old New' synagogue. Tiny deep-set windows connect the main body of the synagogue, where the renowned Rabbi Loew used to sit, with the vestibule where the women sat to peer at the proceedings.

Nearby are the jagged tombs of the cemetery in which many of the stones are engraved with motifs, such as a pair of hands reaching upwards. The cemetery was established in 1587 and was used up until the end of the eighteenth century, by which time there were up to nine layers of graves.

The ceremonial hall of the cemetery now houses a museum to the Jewish children of Czechoslovakia, about fifteen thousand of whom perished in the death camp of Terezin. Four thousand drawings survive from these dead children, many of whom became remarkably politically acute in their years of imprisonment before final execution. Some of them gathered together to publish a magazine, optimistically entitled 'We lead'. The editor was fourteen years old. Many of their drawings are curiously divorced from the horror of their surroundings and depict dogs, rabbits and butterflies in green fields. Others are pervaded with symbols of fear, boiling pots, black devils and children lying in coffins.

The decision of the enlightened empress to abolish the ghetto dispersed the talent of the Jewish community over the city. In the Golden Lane behind the Hradcany Castle is a minute cottage, now used for the sale of souvenirs and records, where Franz Kafka was born. The writings of the most renowned author to have come out of Prague are not officially approved and his memory is scarcely acknowledged. It is not merely the satirical content of his writings that have failed to win him official approval, but the fact that, like most of his Jewish compatriots, he spoke and wrote in German.

PRAGUE

Departure

'THE PEOPLE OF Czechoslovakia are in chains, chains made of sausages,' mused the old man. He was repling to my question why the political situation in Prague seemed to move in circles rather than progress in any particular direction. He lived in a gently disordered apartment on the outskirts of Prague, surrounded by shelves-full of Orwell, Joyce and Hemingway. He was a dissident, one of the leaders of the Charter Seventy-Seven movement. His conversation reminded me what a small world was Prague. He spoke with love and deep dislike of Masaryk and Gottwald, of the Sudeten Germans and the Jews, with the familiarity of one who had known them all.

The old man was right about the easy nature of Czechoslovakia's chains. It was a glorious mid-summer's day. The sun reflected on the buttons of the policemen stationed in Wenceslas Square. Prague gleamed as brightly as a new pin. Every façade glistened with freshly applied paint. Everywhere there was paint, paint, paint.

In the Obneci Dum, which looked like a Cunard liner, the huge hall was filled from morning to night, and not only with tourists. In the café Europa on Wenceslas Square a string quartet was playing. Copies of *Morning Star* were strewn over the tables, under the art nouveau lamps. I spotted what I took to be a young lady with a thick mane of red hair. When she looked up, however, I could see that she was at least eighty years old, wearing a wig that might have been borrowed from the dressing room of Lucille Ball. Three captivated German students crossed the floor to pay homage to this lone survivor of bohemian Bohemia. She was quite delighted by the attention and offered the first a tiny white hand for him to kiss.

The cafés of Prague are always full, perhaps because those who patronise them are served incredibly slowly by the slovenly and disagreeable waitresses. The tardy arrival of these vixens rarely brought me any satisfaction. The menus were thrown at me like fish to a seal. Tipping was universally expected and universally on a grand scale, though the usual acknowledgment for this was no more than a grunt. A request for tea once resulted in lemonade. A cappucino? It was an Irish coffee, stone cold, probably prepared the day before. Chocolate cake? Yes, of course. On came the profiteroles.

There was no sign of the health fad which has most of western Europe and America in its grip, which was surprising in a nation which took up sport clubs with such a vengeance in the nineteenth century, in an effort to outstrip the Germans in brawn if not in brain. Perhaps the expulsion of the Germans had made it unnecessary. Chocolate cakes, brandy and cigarettes maintained their ascendancy even at the breakfast table. At luncheon, vegetables maintained only a symbolic presence. A sliver of cabbage; a small hillock of onion.

The cafés of Prague are the scenes of loitering and loving. Many of the customers are tourists, recovering from the dazzling rudeness of the Czech tourist officials. Many are also Praguers, staring blankly at the wall, lazily chasing a piece of chocolate cake around the plate.

There appears to be more time for love in Prague than in most countries. One does not notice this phenomenon in hectic western cities, where frantic bouts of snatched sex are more appropriate to people engaged in a competitive rat race. In Prague there is much more time for such things and romance blooms. This does not spill over into official encounters. The camp smirks and over-ripe smiles of the waiters and waitresses of East Berlin seem a very long way in this city of public snarls. In the parks and cafés of Prague, however, one is struck by the ubiquity of lovers, who have occupied each available seat and stare at each other with complete adoration for hours are a time.

I enjoyed two memorable meals in Prague. U Pinkasu is a well known old tavern where one can eat well and cheaply. I had just ordered my meal when an elderly American sitting next to me suddenly turned and half shouted, 'I ain't never kissed the earth, but I'm sure gonna kiss it when I get out of this goddammed country.'

'I gather you are not enjoying your holiday.'

'Ain't never prayed in a church in me life but I'm sure as hell gone to pray to God when I get out of this fucking country.'

Then he added: 'Seen them whores on the main drag?'

I said that all I had seen was a great many policemen.

'Nigger pimps the lot of 'em. Too old to go for 'em meself, so just watch yourslf.'

My last meal in Prague was in the Prazcka restaurant in Karlovaz, a small eating place specialising in excellent steaks. When I arrived it was quite empty and the blinds were drawn although it was midday.

'Would you mind sitting here?' said the patron. He directed me past a camera on a tripod, from which issued a mass of cables, towards a perfectly arranged table for one.

'We are taking publicity photographs,' he explained.

I ordered my steak as the camera was wheeled in front of me. A cassette of Marilyn Monroe singing 'I wanna be loved by you' began to play, perhaps to put me at my ease. The waiter positioned himelf behind me with a bottle in hand and wore the kind of jovial smile I had never otherwise encountered in Prague. I cut my steak into neat strips, smiling vaguely at the camera while my eyes were blinded by the popping of flash lights.

WROCŁAW

News from Potsdam

THE TRAIN RUMBLED and swayed through hissing rain in a dark Bohemian night. After we crossed the frontier between Poland and Czechoslovakia, the Polish family who had been sitting opposite me in complete silence started clapping. They passed round Smarties and boiled sweets to everyone in the compartment, which immediately came to life through the unconscious relief we all clearly felt on leaving Czechoslovakia.

The train to Wrocław did not leave Prague until 6.50 in the evening, however, which meant that I was due to arrive in Poland at the inconvenient time of half past two in the morning. After the momentary euphoria of leaving Prague had died down, I was full of regret that I had not taken the trouble to reserve a single hotel room in Poland.

The officials at the Polish tourist board in London had laughed with scorn at the idea of booking rooms in advance. Their London office was managed by a tall, well built man dressed in bell-bottoms with a round face that was framed by a shock of lank blond hair.

He had completed my visa requirements whilst talking to his girl friend on the telephone at the same time.

'How long will you be in Poland, fourteen days?... Oh excuse me. Yeah, liquid night last night... uh huh, about four in the morning, . . . yeah, feeling ropy . . .'

When the visa was ready, he dismissed the subject of hotel rooms with a wave of his hand.

'Why bother?' he said with a smile. 'With your western money you will live like a king! Find something when you get there . . . excuse me again. Uh huh, Lindy was there too . . . uh huh, still fighting with Eric? . . .'

It seemed a strange way for a tourist office to carry on, but I dismissed it as an example of Polish waywardness. Finally he put down the phone.

'Incidentally, have you heard about the price of women in Warsaw? Two hundred dollars a night. They're the most expensive girls in the world.'

As I left he left me with one last piece of advice. 'There's a lot of mugging nowadays in Warsaw. Last week I heard about someone who was mugged before they had even got out of the airport.'

At half past two I was awoken from a deep sleep in the Polish family opposite. 'Wrocław!' the husband shouted in my ear, shaking me hard by the shoulder to wake me up. I stumbled drowsily out of the carriage, dragging my black suitcase behind me.

The station was full of people. Through blurred eyes, the waiting-room seemed bathed in white light. I smelt alcohol fumes. The station was full of people, many of whom seemed to be drunk. I was struck by the numbers who were travelling in the middle of the night.

Pulling my suitcase behind me along the cobbled streets outside the station, as if it was a recalcitrant pet dog, I discovered a hotel that was open. At a quarter past three I went to sleep. The telephone beside my bed rang at half past four.

'I forgot to tell you,' the receptionist announced breathlessly. 'Breakfast is served from seven o'clock in the morning onwards!'

'Thanks very much!' I shouted back, slamming down the receiver. I slept until eleven. Then, as it was Sunday and I was in Poland, I went to Mass.

Wrocław was a disconcerting city. After alighting from the train in the vast mock-gothic railway station, my eyes blurred by the white lights of the street lamps, I had a sudden feeling that I was back in Germany. The gothic town hall looked German. So did the steep-roofed churches and the squares lined with gabled *burgermeisters'* houses.

Wrocław was a stage set for a German production. But I soon discovered that the cast were all Polish. The signs over the coffee houses said *kawarnia*. The noticeboards pinned to the doors of the steep-roofed churches and which I half expected to detail a twice-weekly Lutheran *gottesdienst* instead detailed an unending list of Mass timetables in Polish. I tried making a few enquiries for directions in German and was answered by incomprehending stares.

The Silesian metropolis of Breslau was the greatest single casualty of the redrawing of Europe's boundaries which was undertaken by the Allies at their various conferences in Teheran, Yalta and Potsdam between 1943 and 1945.

Stalin had determined on incorporating the old Polish city of Lvov into the Ukraine as part of the spoils of victory. Under intense pressure from Churchill, the Polish Prime Minister in exile, Mikolajczyk, was forced to accede to Stalin's demand. Churchill thereby hoped, in vain as it turned out, to 'save' the rest of Poland from falling under Soviet influence. The decision to incorporate Lvov into the Soviet Union, however, left its Polish citizens with nowhere to live.

The news from the Potsdam Conference of the Allied victors in 1945 was that Poland would be generously compensated by the annexation of German lands to the west. To be precise: 'The former German territories east of a line running from the Baltic Sea immediately west of Swinemünde and thence along the Oder river to the confluence of the western Neisse river ... shall be under the administration of the Polish state.'

The Polish frontier moved one hundred and fifty miles westwards to absorb East Prussia, Pomerania and Silesia, which had been integral members of the heartland of Germany since the twelfth century. The city of Breslau was wiped off the map of Europe by the stroke of a pen. The inhabitants packed their bags and were evacuated to fend for themselves amid the rubble of post-war Berlin – those who did not die on the way. The empty city was repopulated with Poles, many of whom were displaced refugees from Lvov. An entirely new Polish city was founded in the ruins of Breslau. It was named 'Wrocław'.

Armed with this uncomfortable knowledge, Breslau or Wrocław's eeriness was understandable. The familiarity of its German architecture brought no consolation. On the contrary, it was like meeting and old and familiar friend who had undergone a lobotomy and had forgotten even how to speak his native language. It gave me a premonition of how it would be to return to London after a long absence only to discover that everyone there now spoke Gaelic and that the last thousand years of history had simply been erased not only from the textbooks but from people's consciousness.

There was no compromise between old Germany and new Poland in Wrocław. Every sign and tombstone that pointed towards the age when Wrocław was 'Breslau' had been removed. Only the buildings themselves remained to protest silently their German origins.

To dress up this shocking alteration in the rags of historical righteousness, a great many books and tracts were published by the presses of the Polish government which documented the presence of Slavic tribes around Wrocław in the misty years of the tenth and eleventh centuries. Henceforth, the lands of Prussia, Silesia and Pomerania were officially referred to as the 'recovered territories'. It is rather as if Denmark had justified the annexation, or the 'recovery', of the eastern counties of England around Norwich on the grounds that they had once formed the patrimony of King Canute.

In the restaurants and cafés of Wrocław, I realised that Poland lay on the other side of an economic wall which was higher, more insurmountable and somehow much more depressing than the Wall made of bricks and barbed in Berlin. In comparison to the wall between the west and Poland, the Berlin Wall appeared to be little more than a statement of intention; a public announcement that from this point eastwards things were going to get worse.

The drama of crossing from East to West Berlin was not very lasting. Like all superb theatre props, the impression given by the Berlin Wall was deep but transient. Behind the seriousness of all that sabre-rattling by the armed guards pointing rifles from their watchtowers, the Berlin which lay to the east of the wall was not very different from the Berlin which lay to the west.

There was the initial shock of East Berlin's pervasive greyness, but I quickly adjusted to seeing the world in black and white tones and to the necessity of queuing for my afternoon coffee. In spite of the very different roads taken by the two Germanies after the war, every pore of East Germany proclaimed its adherence to the solid, protestant, respectably 'bourgeois' world from which I had come. From the other side of the Wall, East Germany seemed no more alien than the England of the late 1940s in the period of austerity.

Nor did East Germany appear to be a country that was at odds with its own history. In a highly idiosyncratic way, it had bound together some tangled threads of its own choosing from Luther's Saxony, Frederick the Great's Prussia and the Weimar Republic and it had rather convincingly claimed them as its own.

In Prague I had the definite feeling that doors were silently closing behind me without my noticing. The food was varied and plentiful. The cafés rejoiced in a comfortingly familiar central European ambience. But Prague was palpably squirming with some kind of internal discomfort, like someone who had swallowed a stone and could not get rid of it. In Prague the break with the past had been too savage to make the present comprehensible, let alone tolerable. Everywhere there were nerve ends that lay exposed, twitching and fizzing angrily.

I sat in my *kawarnia*, furiously chewing a dismal bun and angrily waving away a persistent fly. Wrocław had brought me up short. Having cooly jumped over several walls since leaving West Berlin, I had seen no reason why I should not be able to jump over another in Poland. But in Wrocław I felt as if I had attempted to jump over a wall and had crashed right into the brickwork instead. The change in lifestyle was so drastic that I took it as a personal offence. Between me and West Berlin, the Wall had grown higher not by feet but by yards.

History had been turned upside down. Who was in charge of history? I wanted to lodge a complaint. Wrocław even looked as pinched and starved as one of those failed businessmen who have lately taken to sleeping in their best suits under a bridge. There were clearly to be no more idle afternoons spent in snug cafés. My *kawarnia* was as inviting as a nineteenth-century workhouse with a menu that suited the surroundings.

A pervasive sense of decay clung like poison ivy to the stately burghers' houses outside the *kawarnia* in the square. Many had crumbled into a gentle decay where they had not actually collapsed. Only the churches were in good repair.

In spite of the concentration of churches in the city centre, at least half of which would have been converted into social clubs if they were in England, each one that I passed appeared to be crowded to capacity with worshippers on Sunday morning.

The streets outside the churches were sabbath-empty. On the way to the cathedral, the sounds of the Polish Mass mingled with the more sonorous chanting of eastern-rite catholics. These catholics who follow the rites of the orthodox church were once numerous in Lvov and their descendants still enjoy the use of several churches in Wrocław. In one of these churches, where the Lutheran piety of Breslau had given way to the incense and icons of Wrocław, there was a magnificent womens' choir led by a stout middle-aged lady who was conducting her sisters from a balcony at the back of the church.

At the door of the cathedral, one Mass was ending and another was beginning when I arrived. A medieval scene: nuns in old-fashioned pointed wimples, which obscured their faces, bustled through the throng of people waiting outside the door of the cathedral, where beggars supplicated meekly for the alms of the faithful.

The side ambulatories of the cathedral were almost pitch dark owing to the murky quality of the stained glass. Families had grouped themselves around the altars in the side chapels to recite their private devotions in the darkness, which made the ambulatory sound like a whispering gallery.

Eerie Wrocław. The town hall square was empty on a Sunday afternoon, except for a small group of people who had gathered around two comedians from Hamelin. Two policemen from the 'Milicja' stood by motionless, basking in the wan rays of the afternoon sun. The comedians from Hamelin were receiving the warm applause of the crowd, along with a considerable amount of money, for the Poles are generous to the core.

A young man dressed as the Mad Hatter appeared suddenly from nowhere. He honked noisly on a large horn, and ran around in several small circles like a dog chasing its tail. Then he disappeared honking furiously down a side street. The two 'Milicja' stood and stared.

This curious and inconsequential event may have had something to do with the so-called 'Orange People' in Wrocław. Wrocław is a young city, populated by the children of the evacuees of Lvov, with a high proportion of students. The city has inherited Lvov's radical and artistic mantle in the new Poland. Wrocław has a particular reputation as a centre for radical alternative groups like the 'Orange People', who have taken to subverting the social order by unconventional means. They stage inexplicable events which they call 'happenings' (the English word is always used) whose political intent is concealed by a mad-cap veneer.

The comedians continued playing in the town hall square. It was then that I noticed that the four phone booths which had been entirely empty when I last looked round had silently filled up with so many young people that their arms and legs were hanging out of the doors like the tentacles of an octopus. The two members of the 'Milicja' standing a little way off looked at their boots with embarrassment.

'Hey ... Milicja!' came a single, sarcastic-sounding voice from one of the booths. The two comedians from Hamelin were now juggling balls to the delight of the children in the audience.

'Milicja' looked up uneasily and shifted from one boot to another, obviously unwilling to approach the phone booths in front of the crowd watching the jugglers. The four phone booths broke into a single chant of 'Solidarnosc' for a minute. Then the occupants darted away as noiselessly as they came.

I went back to my hotel, disconcerted by Wrocław.

CRACOW

Wawel Hill

IF A COUNTRY can be said to have a physical heart, then the heart of Poland surely lies betwixt the Royal Castle and the cathedral on Cracow's Wawel Hill. The cathedral contains forty-one of the forty-five tombs of the kings of Poland. Their funerary monuments, such as that of John III, 'Electioni Polonico, Lithuanico, Prussico, liberatione Austriatico Pannonico, profligatione Ottomanico...' do something to evoke the power, the pride and the glory of the kingdom of Poland before it was partitioned in the eighteenth century between Austria, Russia and parvenu Prussia.

Galicia, the Grand Duchy of Cracow and the Duchy of Teschen escaped the tyranny of Berlin and St Petersburg for the more benign neglect of the Empress Theresa's Austria. The empress was the most reluctant of the three to partition Poland. 'She wept,' it was said. 'She took, but she wept.' In Austrian Poland, centred on Cracow, the Poles were eventually permitted a good deal of autonomy. In 1861 a Galician Diet was established, though its conservative flavour was guaranteed by the preponderance of bishops, archbishops, the rectors of the universities of Cracow and Lvov, and a number of landlords.

Cracow cathedral was begun in the 1020s. Most of the present structure dates from the fourteenth century. Unlike the cathedral in

Berlin, Cracow's cathedral was more than a resting place for the royal family. Cracow is hallowed by the great silver shrine of Saint Stanisław, Bishop of Cracow and martyr. Stanisław was assassinated in 1079 on the orders of King Boleslaw and, like Thomas à Becket, he was subsequently canonised. His baroque silver sarcophagus, embellished with details of the bishop's life and martyrdom and surmounted by cherubs bearing the episcopal mitre and crosier, was wrought by the Danzig silversmith, Peter van Rennen.

The Poles do not revile the founding father of their present independence in the same unpleasant way that the Czechs either officially ignore or besmirch the name of their first leader, Thomas Masaryk. In the crypt of Wawel cathedral, the flag of Poland is draped over the tomb of Josef Pilsudski, the man who forged Polish independence in 1918 and then presided over the so-called 'miracle of the Vistula' in 1920, when Trotsky's Red Army was repelled from the gates of Warsaw.

At Cracow station I asked the taxi-driver to take me to the room-finding service of the tourist bureau. The taxi-driver was a chatty septuagenarian with a shock of white hair, who introduced himself as Neumann. He said that his family called him 'Opa', German for Grandpa. I asked him whether he was Polish or German. 'Neither. My father was an Austrian soldier stationed in Cracow and my mother was Polish.'

He drew up outside a grey and indistinguishable tenement, which, as I objected, did not resemble a tourist bureau.

'It isn't, it's my son's place, which is much better. Bathroom, bedroom, big hall, yours for only 10,000 złoty a night, or three dollars if you prefer.'

I agreed to take a look, upon which Opa shouted up the stairs 'Andrej!' and a burly young man came hurtling down followed by a woman with long brown hair wound into a careless pigtail. With not so much as a by-your-leave, the two of them grabbed my luggage and made off with it at lightning speed up the stairs. It appeared that I was staying at the Neumanns.

'Good,' said the old man. 'Now, how about changing some money? Dollars, deutschmarks, pounds...? How about a trip to Auschwitz?' he continued briskly. He made it sound like a trip to the seaside.

I murmured something about having already been to Lidice, in Czechoslovakia. 'You can't stay in Cracow without a trip to Auschwitz,' Opa retorted dismissively. '17,000 złotys return trip, or five dollars. Whichever you prefer.'

While Opa was working I kept company with his son, who spoke no German and only six words in English. These were 'Rubbish, Germany, strip-tease, money, pope and stop', which he used with great ingenuity. When his youngest daughter, a five-year-old minx by the name of Beata and clearly the apple of her father's eye, disrupted our late-night drinking sessions, he would chase her round the room waving a belt and shouting 'Stop that rubbish strip-tease!' She had heard it many times before and squealed with delight.

Andrej liked to doodle maps of Europe on those rainy afternoons when we would all sit together in the front room. He would draw a circle, label it 'Polska' and surround it by hostile arrows labelled DDR, CSSR and USSR. Sometimes he got it into his head that we ought to have a conversation together in German and would bound into the kitchen, rummage around for the huge German dictionary that lived under the stove, and then return with his prize under one arm. These expeditions in search of a common language were invariably fruitless. He would search feverishly in the dictionary for the word he wanted, for about ten seconds, only to fling the book on the floor with mock disgust and laugh.

The Neumanns were one of those Polish families who, on the strength of a surname, had lately decided they were in fact German. I found this vaguely distressing. I was raised on the assumptions of the mawkishly salovophile English press. To me the word 'Poland' was connected with such adjectives as 'indomitable' and 'semper fidelis'. The Neumann's enthusiasm for offering round trips to Auschwitz seemed somehow indecent. A country which had suffered so much at German hands in the last war ought, I felt, to cherish a little modest hatred for the hereditary Teutonic foe, which as a fellow Teuton I could sympathise with without enjoining. But two of Opa Neumann's children had already left for the city of Essen in West Germany, which Opa Neumann described in much the same terms as those reserved by orthodox Jews for Jersusalem. After a hard day of taxi-driving and arranging deals with foreign tourists, Opa liked nothing better than to push back his chair, pour a large vodka, iron out his habitual frown into a sweet smile and discourse about the Promised Land to the west where the streets were paved with gold.

This *bonhomie* was reserved exclusively for West Germans and Austrians. The East Germans he regarded as counterfeits, the worst kind of impostors. 'They're not just communist on the skin, they're communist in the *head*,' he would say, tapping his big skull.

I sometimes chided him about the way he lionised the West Germans. 'So go and live in Essen yourself,' I once said. Then Opa rubbed his chin and said, 'Not yet, not yet, so much to do,' and pointed with a sigh at Andrej and his huge brood of children (there was another on the way). Poor Andrej was a shambles in comparison with his father, almost toothless and scarcely recognisable from the handsome blade in the wedding photograph on the wall.

Opa Neumann had an irritating habit, which became more apparent after I had been in Cracow for a week or so. He would lie in wait for me to return from the day's sightseeing and, as soon as I closed the front door, would lauch off into how many dollars he had paid for a couple of sparkplugs for the car, how two Yugoslav businessmen had given him an immense wad of deutschmarks for delivering them to the apartment of the local prostitute (at this point he would look at me rather hopefully), how televisions now cost half a million złotys and how his son in Essen had just bought a Mercedes. But Opa Neumann's multifarious dealings had undoubtedly made him into one of the wealthier citizens in Cracow (half the wealth of Poland seemed to be concentrated in the hands of bellhops, waiters or taxi-drivers). He had privately bought two flats in Cracow alone. So when he ended each of these speeches, with the rhetorical question 'How can we live?' I always longed to answer, 'Quite well, it seems.'

The flat was not the bargain Opa promised. Opa, Andrej, Mrs Neumann and the six children camped like refugees in the front room, which made expeditions from the bedrooms to the bathroom extremely hazardous, especially at night, when my big feet inevitably landed on some small Neumann. In the daytime the bathroom was perpetually occupied by Mrs Neumann and her vast piles of washing, which she would fling into a great barrel and which, when it span, sounded like an aircraft engine. But the greatest surprise was, upon returning from dinner one evening, discovering a German deaconess called Juta whom Opa had double booked into my bedroom. The deaconess had evidently received no more warning about her shared quarters than I had, for she opened her mouth in astonishment as Opa struggled in with a second mattress and said, 'Plenty of room for two here' before hurriedly disappearing.

Below Wawel Hill, Cracow converges on the Rynek, a large square with an arcaded cloth-hall, on the edge of which is the church of St Mary. From the church tower a trumpet sounds every hour. The last note is always curtailed in memory of a fourteenth-century watchman who was felled in mid-blast by the arrow of a Tatar. The interior of the church is dark, so that the great fifteenth-century folding relief on the high altar is difficult to appreciate at first. A small nun opened the folding sides for my benefit, to the accompaniment of classical music, to reveal six scenes in the life of Christ decorated in brilliant paint and gold leaf. It is the work of Wit Stwosz, who was relieved of all taxes and dues by the grateful city fathers. Even on a midweek afternoon it was difficult to tour the church owing to the number of worshippers, and I felt uncomfortably profane in concentrating so overtly on the artwork whilst an elderly priest in an old cotta and stole heard confessions from a row of women who were waiting patiently in a line beside the confessional.

On the other side of the square is the tower of the town hall, no longer, alas, attached to the town hall, which was dismantled in the nineteenth century. It was completed in 1383 and suffered a number of fires in the sixteenth and seventeenth centuries. The cupola was replaced in the 1780s. The beautiful room on the first floor was once the chapel of the town councillors. Above are smaller rooms affording an excellent view of the square and which house an exhibition of photographs of the city in the last century.

The Rynek cloth-hall is said to contain one of the best cafés in Poland. The pantheon of celebrated former patrons include Lenin, who whiled away some of his idler hours here playing chess. But years of shortages have made havoc of Poland's menus. They were, no doubt, printed years ago in Bulgaria as part of some Comecon agreement, as they seemed no different from those I saw in East Germany or Czechoslovakia. The waitress seemed amused when I ordered fried eggs and ham, and answered with a well worn 'Nie.'

'In that case I'll have an omelette,' I said with an accommodating smile. The answer was negative. I then poked a finger at several items, with an increasingly worried expression, but I noticed that the waitress was now looking at the ceiling with embarrassment. Clearly none of the items on the menu was currently available.

'Tea?' I inquired in a small voice. She nodded.

'And milk?'

'Nie!'

'Black tea it is,' I concluded sorrowfully.

The Neumanns were shouting at each other about the price of sugar when I returned. 'There's going to be shortage so we're going to buy the lot up,' confided Opa. They were also shouting at Juta, the German deaconess, about the pictures on our bedroom wall. Juta, who I discovered with trepidation was not West German but East German, had delivered me a long and serious sermon the previous evening about her difficulties with the East German church and about her own private campaign for feminist theology to be taught in the theology faculty at Leipzig. I could guess, therefore, what had become the rock of offence between her and the Neumanns. On one wall of our bedroom was an innocuous Madonna. But on the other were displayed the ample charms of Samantha Fox and those of another sultry lady by the name of Sabrina.

'These pictures are coming off,' Juta announced as she briskly removed Samantha and Sabrina from the wall, while Opa looked on angrily from the open doorway. Mrs Neumann alone seemed indifferent to the dispute over Sabrina. She was off out the door with a wad of dollars and deutschmarks with which she intended to buy up Cracow's supply of sugar.

Opa took me aside that evening in the living room, leaving Juta to stew in the sanitised juice of the bedroom. He poured us both a couple of beers. 'A *woman* priest!' he sneered, translating this news into Polish for the benefit of the rest of the family.

Mrs Neumann shook her head sorrowfully. '*And* she is *East* German,' he continued, his voice shaking with the self-righteous indignation of a Victorian clergyman who had discovered that the housemaid was pregnant. 'If I'd known she was from the DDR, I would *never* have let her into the house. I thought she was from the West! Incidentally, you haven't said whether you want the trip to Auschwitz.

CRACOW

Auschwitz

'Everything proceeds in a perfectly orderly fashion.'

From a report on Auschwitz delivered in May 1941 by SS Stuermbannfuehrer
Francke-Gricksch to the Head of SS Main Personnel

IN THE MUSEUM cinema at Auschwitz, the light of the projector that was showing a crackly old documentary film on the liberation of the camp by the Allies in 1945 fell onto a bare auditorium. The room was empty with the exception of two small heads silhouetted against the screen towards the front. I was more interested in these two lonely looking pilgrims than in the contents of the film, so I seated myself in the front row to observe them. They were both blonde, tanned and athletic in appearance, as classically Aryan as one could wish. I turned back to the screen to catch sight of the old Polish communist leader in the 1940s, Bierut, striding around and waving to an enthusiastic crowd. My eyes then strayed leftwards once more. These two were Germans undoubtedly, but what had brought them here, to the scene of the crime, as it were? I took in worried expressions, then their vaguely unfashionable clothes, the intelligent but apologetic cast of expression, of people who are well-versed in the art of saying sorry. As the film drew to a close I itemised my conclusions. East German without a doubt. Youngish, liberal in opinions, professionals, living in a big city like Berlin or Leipzig. Purpose of visit? Dutifully and joylessly discovering at first hand the sins of their fathers.

The film over, I followed Dagmar and Baronius, as they were called, out of the auditorium and into the rain.

'No, not Berlin. Karl Marx Stadt. Doctors, yes, both of us. No, no children.'

We trudged down the gravel paths towards the gas ovens in silence.

Auschwitz-Birkenau, to give the camp its complete name, has been preserved in its entirety as a museum, to provide a salutary warning to future generations of the bloody bathos entailed within that innocuous phrase, 'just obeying orders'. The flower beds beside the crematoria are as carefully tended today as they were in the time of the camp's wartime commandant, Rudolf Hoess. Over the gateway there is still suspended the ironic and deceitful sign proclaiming in German, 'Arbeit macht Frei', 'work brings freedom'.

Quite deserted in the rain apart from the two Germans and myself, Auschwitz less resembled a museum than the abandoned shrine of an evil deity, a kind of cathedral erected to the glory of the German Shiva-the-destroyer, who blasted his way with such demonic strength over Poland in 1939.

In this particular house of sacrifices, several million human beings – the precise number is unknown – were gassed and burnt on insatiable burning altars. And here the descendants of the artisans who worked with such disturbing sensitivity on perfecting the human expressions of the delicate images in Erfurt cathedral perpetuated atrocities the gross savagery of which is unparelleled in the known history of Europe.

'False teeth,' said Baronius. 'Piles of false teeth.'

Inside the halls, where prisoners once languished on ratty pallets, the debris abandoned by the Nazi guards during their hurried evacuation of the camp has been left as an exhibition behind glass panels. Behind one panel is a pile of hair and behind another a collection of toothbrushes. Each inanimate object harbours some ghastly secret, some particle of the story of which only small horrific fragments survive today. I stared at the pile of spectacle rims, then at a mound of children's toys.

Auschwitz-Birkenau was established in 1941 as the largest concentration camp in the German-occupied territories of eastern Europe with the task of executing Hitler's order for the 'final solution' to the 'question of the Jews'. Four vast gas chambers gave Auschwitz the means of outdoing Treblinka, Belsen, Sibibor and Chelmoin the capacity to destroy human life, at a rate of nearly 10,000 every twenty-four hours.

According to Francke-Gricksch's report, 'the most advanced methods permit the execution of the Fuehrer's order in the shortest possible time and without arousing much attention' in Auschwitz. The most important method was the use of Zyklon B gas, a prussic acid which, after its discovery in 1941, was pronounced a more efficient, economical method of killing people than noisy, cumbersome and expensive firing squads. Francke-Gricksch described the use of Zyklon B gas at Auschwitz for the benefit of his curious superiors:

> The prisoners ... go down 5 or 6 steps into a fairly long, well-constructed and well-ventilated cellar area, which is lined with benches to the left and right. It is brightly lit and the benches are numbered. The prisoners are told that they are to be cleansed and disinfected for their assignments. They must therefore be completely undressed to be bathed. To avoid panic and prevent disturbances of any kind, they are instructed to arrange their clothes neatly under their respective numbers so that they will be able to find their things again after their bath. Everything proceeds in a perfectly orderly fashion ... then they pass through a small corridor and enter a large cellar room, which resembles a shower bath ... when three or four hundred people have been herded into the room, the doors are shut and containers filled with the substances are dropped into the pillars ... a few minutes later the hair of the corpses is cut off, the teeth extracted ... the corpses are loaded into elevators and brought up to the first floor where ten large crematoria are located ....

Afterwards, inside the gas chamber other Jewish prisoners were given the ghoulish task of disentangling the bodies, which were invariably mangled following the frantic struggles to escape. One guard recalled 'the frantic banging and pounding on the door' of the prisoners when they realised they were not to be bathed but killed and the accompanying jest of the Nazi attendant that 'the water in the shower room must be very hot today' to cause such a furore. Sometimes the Jewish guards had also to clear away the human debris that resulted from the occasional sprees of violence perpetuated by the Nazi guards against dead bodies that were presumably now beyond any further degradation. One guard named Max Hasner recalled discovering the bodies of seventy Jewish women whose breasts had all been torn off or mutilated by the guards: 'The courtyard sloped steeply and the drains became blocked with blood. We were wading in blood up to our ankles.'

Every cult attracts its own mad enthusiasts, like the 'Beast of Belsen' and the Nazi guard at Auschwitz whose favourite trick was to suspend one of the prisoners, hands bound to feet, over a pole and deal him blows of such force that the prisoner's body spun round its axis in a complete revolution. These practices have received a great deal of publicity, partly on account of the fascination of the general public in the perverse profundity of these crimes and partly, one suspects, because the idea that Auschwitz was staffed by evil lunatics allows the rest of us to draw a veil between this bestial aberration and our own more rational world. The camp museum perpetuates this view by displaying a room full of cartoons depicting scenes of daily life in Auschwitz in which prisoners are gratuitously tortured by Nazi guards whose faces have been so distorted as to resemble animals rather than people.

It is comforting, I suppose, to imagine that tyrannies like that of Hitler are supported by a kind of subspecies of human that creeps out from under the stones for the occasion, as it absolves the rest of us from much responsibility. But one fears the truth is less dramatic and more sinister. One fears that the vast majority of the staff at Auschwitz were no more insane than the average unthinking civil servant and that behind much of their cruelty lay a kind of ruthless logic, rather than sadism. There were no doubt some SS guards who truly enjoyed picking out children for the gas chambers in Auschwitz, but most seem to have competed for this task on account of the extra cigarettes and other rations awarded to those who took part in this particular task. Killing kids equals extra cigs. It was as simple, as devastatingly simple, as that for much of the time.

The charge of insanity could hardly be levelled at the camp's commandant, Rudolf Hoess, who as a youth had been vaguely pious and even harboured notions of joining the Roman Catholic priesthood before opting instead for the superior discipline of the Nazi party. Whilst the ovens of Auschwitz worked day and night to cremate up to 10,000 people a day (pumping so much thick smoke into the night sky that, as Hoess later recalled, it created a 'terrible stench' in the surrounding villages) Hoess insisted on the diligent maintenance of the flower beds surrounding the crematoria and encouraged those who were soon to die clawing at the sealed doors of the shower room to occupy themselves in the meantime with the formation of choral music groups.

There was nothing even faintly insane about the intense, one might say snug, relationship that was built up between Auschwitz-Birkenau and several captains of German industry. For the directors of I.G. Farben chemical works and the Krupp armament empire, the supply of disposable slaves supplied by Auschwitz came as something of a godsend. What could possibly be better than a limitless supply of workers who could be kept toiling away until they were exhausted and then replaced immediately by a fresh batch? The children had to go, however, 'invariably exterminated', as Commandant Hoess recalled, 'since by reason of their youth they were unable to work'.

The factories employing labour from Auschwitz were not the only ones with a finger in the pie. I.A. Topf and Sons of Erfurt were the fortunate recipients of the contract to build the gas ovens at Auschwitz. Degesch, short for German Pest Control Ltd, were the profitable purveyors of Zyklon B gas. Other companies benefited from the sales of human products by the Auschwitz authorities, such as human hair for the production of wigs and upholstery. Teeth, however, remained the private preserve of the SS. The gold fillings were deposited in the Reichsbank in Berlin under an account in the name of 'Max Heiliger', following a private agreement between Himmler and the Reichsbank President.

I never told Opa and my hosts in Cracow that I had secretly made the trip to Auschwitz, though I paid dearly for it by being subjected to regular nagging on the subject from Opa. Baronius, Dagmar and I returned together by bus to Cracow. I couldn't help but admire the sense of responsibility which drove them to visit voluntarily a place like Auschwitz. When we arrived in Cracow, Baronius turned and said, 'How about coming for a pizza?' It was the first time we had communicated since leaving the cinema.

CRACOW

Zakopane

'YOU NEED a holiday,' said Opa one morning.

'I am on holiday.'

Opa ignored the comment. 'You should go and spend some time in the hills. In Zakopane. The mountain air is wonderful.'

Perhaps he was right. I was certainly a little weary of Juta's bleak rages and of stepping over eight people just to get to the bathroom in the middle of the night.

'How long will it take by train?'

'Train? Listen, for ten dollars or thirty deutschmarks if you prefer I will take you there myself. I know a wonderful lady who has a beautiful house. You will love it.'

The road from Cracow to Zakopane takes you through some of the most beautiful countryside in Europe. The green hills are dotted with peasants' houses. Some are built in the old style, wood with brightly painted eaves. Most, however, were large Swiss-style chalets.

'Private, every one of them,' commented Opa admiringly. 'The peasants are always complaining but just look at the size of their houses.' In the distance, we could see the high snow-capped peaks of the Tatra mountains bordering Czechoslovakia. At the village of Rabka we passed an old wooden church that could have been in Russia or the Ukraine. We were peceptibly nearing the frontier of catholic Christendom and orthodox Russia.

Opa overtook a couple of East German Wartburg cars chuntering along, which provided him with another opportunity, about the twentieth that week, to vent his spleen against the DDR.

'Just look at those idiots. They are real communists. Communist in the head!' Opa had no kind words for the Czechs either.

'The Slovaks are good people. They're catholic like us. The Hungarians are good fellows as well, but the Czechs! Oh no.'

I began to have the feeling that my life was being arranged with little reference to my own wishes when the car rolled up a sidestreet of Zakopane. Once again, as on my arrival in Cracow, my bags were whisked out of the back and installed inside the house long before their owner. Like some piece of valuable merchandise I had been delivered lock, stock and barrel from one home to another.

I should have smelled a rat when Opa told me of the wonderful address he had lined up for me in Zakopane. I was already entertaining dreams of a little wooden cottage in the hills where I would be looked after by some pious and motherly old peasant in a headscarf, cooking up omelettes on a roaring old-fashioned range.

'This woman is a marvellous person,' said Opa enthusiastically as he removed my luggage from the boot of the car. 'She's so smart. She has hotels all over Poland, in Zakopane, Gdansk, all over. And *all* private!' My heart sank. The house in front of us was a tasteless modern 'villa' embellished with a hundred tell-tale nick-nacks attesting to the nouveau-riche vulgarity of its owner. There were fake brass lanterns and a patio upon which an unpleasant-looking couple were drinking cocktails. A grey Mercedes lazed in the drive. Crazy paving led up to the door. The doorbell played tunes. A fat middle-aged woman with dyed blonde hair opened it and slapped a couple of hundred złotys smartly into Opa's hand.

'Come, my darling, I am your mama,' she said to me. It was a curious introduction, so I thought it best to proceed to business.

'Opa tells me you would like 8,000 złotys a night for a room.'

'Yes my darling. Only 10,000 złotys a night.'

She was neither deaf nor stupid, so I merely gave Opa a cold glance.

'Very expensive place, Zakopane,' he sighed.

The room in which I was soon installed was a mausoleum to its owner. Over the door was a large black and white portrait of a vivacious blonde in a ball gown, her hair coiled stylishly into a New Look coiffe. Over by the window there was another picture, now in colour, of the same woman, wearing an ostrich-feather scarf. She was holding a baby in church. The face was still vivacious, but it had taken on a venial expression. Underneath the scarlet lips a greedy extra chin had sprouted. I could not help but notice the marked resemblance to Myra Hindley.

On the other wall the baby had grown into a plump girl, one chubby fist curled around a candle. Behind her stood her mother, now extremely overweight and exuding a proprietorial air, very much the same person who had greeted me a few minutes before with such false *bonhomie*.

Zakopane seemed better served with amenities than the other towns I had seen in Poland. The large pedestrian avenue was dotted with cafés and restaurants, the like of which I had not seen since leaving Prague. One nondescript looking establishment called only 'Cocktail bar' served a splendid array of icecreams, including one consisting of four flavours and liberally sprinkled with nuts and fruits of the forest. It seemed most extravagant for Poland. I was so surprised to see such tempting delicacies not only displayed but freely available to anyone who cared to purchase them that when I bought mine I wolfed it down greedily, half suspecting it might be taken away.

On the other side of the street was another café which caught my eye. The menu consisted of bleak whiskies and black teas, but there was an appealing grand piano in the corner upon which a wizened old bird was tinkling away. The performance lasted only a few minutes, after which he paused to look around the cavernous room as if waiting for applause which, however, did not materialise. Wearing a cryptic smile that suggested he did not think his audience worthy of his efforts, he commenced again, but not for long. Every so often he disappeared off for a drink.

At the bottom of the high street, past a nineteenth-century parish church that was constructed in the dreary international mock-gothic style that was imposed by the Roman authorities everywhere from Belgium to India, I discovered the old parish church of Zakopane. It was another wooden structure in the Carpathian style. An evening Mass was being celebrated as I arrived and I pushed through the clustered worshippers, drawn less by the evening celebration than a delicious odour of pine. Although it was but a midweek Mass, the small church was overflowing with summer visitors of all ages. A loudspeaker had been erected in the porch of the church to enable those outside the door to join in the devotions.

The tourists come to Zakopane neither for icecream or even for wooden churches, but for walking. There are cable cars that swing their way up Mount Gwiemont on one side of Zakopane or the High Tatras on the other. From either point one can climb or stroll via several routes, some clearly only suitable for experienced climbers, from the mountain tops back down to the town.

There were no maps available to help tourists like me engage in the activity that provides the principal livelihood for the town. The tourist information centre seemed to regard my request for such a thing as an impertinent interruption to the real work of the day, such as smoking or chatting.

I tried the book shop. What simple connotations that expression has in English! In Zakopane, however, 'trying the bookshop' meant putting aside the best part of a morning for an exercise whose outcome was uncertain. Although it was a large bookshop, some distant pasha had decided that the maximum number of customers who could be allowed into the shop at any one time should be three. The rest of us, about fifty in number, all of whom could have been comfortably accommodated at exactly the same time and could no doubt have completed our business in under five minutes, were forced to wait behind a turnstile and wait for one of the Blessed Trinity inside to emerge and symbolically hand over the shopping basket. I waited for an hour for this Olympic baton to be passed into my waiting hand whilst two twittish schoolgirls held up the proceedings indefinitely by being unable to decide what postcard they wanted to purchase.

I was in! There was an entire counter given over to maps but, naturally, no appropriate maps of the High Tatras other than a curious booklet giving the respective heights of each of the mountains.

For all the daytime bustle, Zakopane offered little in the way of night-life. With some reluctance, therefore, I entered the shabby portals of an establishment by the name of Video Disco, in Krupowski. It was quite clearly a rough and ready sort of place, but as in all eastern

European nightclubs they insist on one reserving a table in advance. This being Poland as opposed to Czechoslovakia, the rule was waived for a foreigner like myself.

At the bar, three drinks were available, gin, vodka and Pepsi. I put in a bid for a gin and tonic, but there was no tonic.

'Gin Pepsi?', the barman suggested hopefully. I decided I could do without a Gin Pepsi and enquired about wine. Yes, this was available. Red? Coming up.

One sip was enough to explain why the barman had initially been so coy about the wine. It was a dreadful compound of port and Cinzano that tasted a little like communion wine. Out of some mad craving for oblivion I not only downed the entire glass but, to the barman's evident surprise, requested another. Half-way down, however, I was overwhelmed not with oblivion but with nausea. Beads of sweat broke out on my forehead as the floor receded and advanced before my eyes. A tell-tale rush of digestive juices into my mouth made it quite clear that within approximately thirty seconds I was about to vomit.

'Come my darling.' It was the next morning. I turned and looked at the alarm clock. Six a.m.

'Come. I am your mama.' No, the words were not intended for me. As I suspected, it was a formula for any prospective customer. Downstairs I could hear a babble of Arabic voices. 'Twenty-eight and twenty-eight makes fifty-six, not seventy-eight,' one of them said in English. There was a pause.

'Yes, yes, my darling. I'm sorry. Come. I am your mama.'

I took the mountain railway up Mount Gubałowska. Gubałowska is ideal terrain for the gentle stroller. The ridge is inhabited all year round. Its emerald green pastures dotted with hayricks in the mellow autumn sunlight made it ressemble a green velvet tapestry embroidered with gold buttons. There were small farmhouses with chickens rooting around on the pathways. I was delighted to find another little wooden church in a spinney. One can walk from the top of Mount Gubałowska to the village of Chochałow, which contains several ancient wooden cottages, but as it was several kilometres away I contented myself with a walk through the meadows, in which several farmers were scything the grass.

It is quite possible to combine a morning walking along the ridge of Gubałowska with an afternoon up Mount Gwiemont. Mount Gwiemont is a great deal higher and altogether sterner and should not be attempted if there is any sign of bad weather. Half way up in the cable car the thick pine forests thin out, before giving way entirely to bare rock. Between Mount Gwiemont and Zakopane are several mysterious, pebble-smooth lakes, locked into the mountains and fed each year, I imagine, by the melting snow of the surrounding peaks. For serious climbers, the cable car up the Tatras is only the starting point for an ascent up the still higher peaks around. For thousands of holiday-makers, however, the trip is made merely for the thrill of gazing down from the grey and windswept peaks at the little collection of matchboxes that is Zakopane. In summer the crowds are so great that one has to get to the bottom of the lift at six or seven in the morning to book a seat if one wants to go up by midday. Once up, they step cautiously along the short ridge and hurry back for a cup of tea in the restaurant before taking the lift down.

I took the shortest and most direct route back down to Zakopane by foot, though the journey still took three and half hours. By the time I arrived it was dark. Summer was clearly over. Cold winds were blowing and it was beginning to rain.

I returned to the house to find a full-scale row going on between 'Mama' and the Arabs (they were Libyans, I discovered). As I changed my clothes I overhear her shouting, 'This is *normal* practice in hotel!' and the Libyans chorusing back, 'No, no, we won't pay!'

I slipped out into the night. There was no going back to the scene of the previous night's embarrassment, so I opted for a small doorway called 'The Empire'. 'Empire' certainly seemed a step up from 'Video Disco' and I was not disappointed. I had not so much as stepped through the door before I was pounced by an eager-looking student of about twenty who escorted me to a seat as if I was a visiting ambassador. I was slightly peeved at not being allowed to use my pitiful Polish vocabulary, but the student seized on my being English with delight.

'No, don't try to order,' he shouted when the waiter came over to ask what I wanted. 'No one here speaks English except me. I will get what you want.' It seemed a bit laborious, but as he was so keen to please, I submitted to this game of Chinese whispers.

'I'll have a beer.'

The message was passed on. Back came the answer. Beer was not available. I didn't want to ruin my evening at the Empire with a glass of wine, so I decided on a whisky. More whispers.

'I'm sorry. The waiter says there are no alcoholic drinks at all at the moment.'

Coffee? No, there was no coffee. Hot chocolate? No. Milk? No. Black tea it was. There was another burst of conversation between the waiter and my interpreter.

'The waiter would like you to try a piece of chocolate cheesecake.'

It wasn't a combination that made me want to get up and dance, so I sipped and munched away desultorily in the corner. Ten minutes later the student came back. 'Still alone!' he said accusingly. 'Who would you like to talk to?' I wasn't quite sure whether I was entitled just to pick out a selection of likely candidates for conversation out of the crowd of teenagers bopping away, so I shrugged helplessly. He stormed purposefully off and returned a short while later leading an embarrassed-looking man to my table by the hand.

'This man speaks English,' the student explained. 'He's called Eric.'

Eric was Dutch and was evidently a bit surprised at being deposited at my table like a piece of booty. The student seemed to suspect that if he was left to himself, Eric might bolt off. He sat down between the two of us and smiled to himself, quite delighted with his match-making, as Eric and I stared silently at each other from opposite ends of the table.

WARSAW

The Hotel Victoria

'MAMA' WAS still snoring as I dragged my suitcase on wheels from the hotel down to Zakopane Station. The train to Warsaw took seven hours. At one station there was a large steam engine hissing gently in a siding. A flock of nuns was waiting on the platform. 'Penguins!' commented the girl sitting opposite me. Her friend laughed uneasily, as if she found the joke a trifle sacreligous.

Between Zakopane and Warsaw I had time to absorb once more the panorama of the Polish countryside, which in the heart of traditional Poland has been less disturbed or altered than elsewhere. It is quite unlike any rural tableau in Europe that I have seen, east or west. The reason is that about 80 per cent of the land remains under the private cultivation of the peasants, most of whom employ the antiquated farming methods used by their grandfathers. As the train rocked and swayed its way through the green Galician countryside, I noticed scarcely any modern equipment or new modern plant, nor even a tractor, for the peasants use horses. They are by no means all poor. If appearances are anything to go by, however, they prefer to invest their money in building large Swiss-style farmsteads where they can accommodate their relatives rather than in purchasing new-fangled machinery. Opa once assured me that most of the peasants of his acquaintance hid their money in chests under the floorboards.

In the late 1940s and early 1950s Poland was dominated by the figure of Bolesław Bierut, under whose leadership Stalin's birthdays were celebrated as if they were national holidays. To such a fervent Muscovite, Poland's peasant farms constituted a stumbling block along the path to true socialism.

The accession of a large area of fertile and well cultivated arable land from the former German territories in particular presented the Polish communists with an opportunity to begin the collectivisation of agriculture on the Soviet model. The experiment in collectivisation failed, however, for even in the late 1940s, Poland was never a blank cheque for the Polish communists in the way that Soviet Russia in the same period became for Stalin. In 1956 the attempt was given up. By then, less than 10 per cent of the land had passed under the management of collective farms.

Then a terrible blow fell upon Bierut. At the historic Twentieth Party Congress of the Soviet Communist Party, the new Soviet leader, Nikita Khrushchev, denounced Stalin's methods as a deviation from the pure gospel of Lenin. It must have been a terrible shock, for upon reading the text of Khrushchev's speech, Bierut expired of a heart attack. The peasants retained their farmsteads and collectivisation never became much of a live issue in Poland.

The countryside looks woefully inefficient, but delightfully human. The patchwork of fields are more varied than one is used to in England. Some strips are fallow, others are ploughed to lay bare the brown soil. Here and there one sees the peasant at work, alone or with his headscarfed wife, hoeing, scything and ploughing with his horse. As it was late summer the fields were dotted with haystacks. Running around the haystacks were a great number of chickens. The peasants' houses are not all picturesque. Many of the richer *kulaks* have built several-storied Swiss chalets, but there are plenty of the older wooden houses left, with painted eaves and windows.

The two girls in my compartment were shorthand typists from Zakopane, off to Warsaw for another term's study. They were full of anecdotes concerning the visit Mr Gorbachev had made to Poland not long before and which had affected little Zakopane quite directly, as the Russian leader's itinerary included a stop-over in the neighbouring village of Pirina, where Lenin spent some of the war years and which commemorates the fact in a Lenin mausoleum. They explained that such was the nervousness of the Zakopane authorities concerning the visit of the great man that they not only repaved the roads in Pirina, but had also repaved the road from Zakopane to the cable car in Kusnice in case the Gorbachevs decided to make an impromptu trip up the mountain. 'We'd been asking for that road to be mended for years. He ought to come to Poland more often,' one of the typists giggled. 'People said they'd even painted the grass.'

Both were convinced that the quality of life was worsening and that there was no future for them in Poland. Neither cared one way or the other for Mr Gorbachev's reforms. I could see why. From the perspective of the average citizen in Poland, these great debates over democratisation and so forth seemed terribly theoretical and remote from everyday life, exciting stuff for poets and film directors, but not much help for the average housewife worrying about the price of bread. One of the girls did not care two hoots for the church either, which was the first time I had encountered such opinions in Poland. 'Actually I'm an atheist,' she remarked, 'but I still go to church when I am home in Zakopane, to show people that I am still a nice girl.'

I arrived in Warsaw at midnight. Wherever I travelled in Poland, it always seemed to involve arriving at the most inconvenient time for booking into a hotel. The sky was black and a gentle rain was drizzling over the illuminated row of tower blocks stretching away from the station. The skyline of East Berlin is punctured by monsters of a similar size and shape. In Berlin, however, a faint whiff of glamour and frivolity attaches itself like ivy to the most unpleasant surroundings. Warsaw by night presented no hint of frivolous and undiscovered pleasures. Only the lights of the sentinel-like outline of the Hotel Forum suggested that here and there, behind the tinted plate-glass windows of an international hotel, there might be small rock-pools of comfort.

After queuing miserably outside the station for a taxi for over an hour, I wondered where on earth I was going to stay. Various shady individuals sidled up in battered old cars and offered to give me a lift, but I had been warned in advance that these makeshift taxis thrived on the cupidity of foreigners, so I hung on grimly at my post.

'Hotel,' I said hopefully, when at last I found an authentic cab.

'Hotel what?' he snapped. This came as something of a disappointment, as I was hoping the taxi driver would supply the answer to this question himself. I was glad to be out of the rain, however. It was warm and I obviously had no intention of getting out until we were at a destination that was not the railway station. I drummed my fingers lightly on the dashboard and said, once more, 'Hotel.'

The taxi driver drove away, grumbling. 'Hotel Saski?' he then suggested, 'Hotel Warszawa? Hotel Forum?' I hesitated.

'Peasant's Home?' he added with a note of desperation. Some answer was called for, if we were not to drive round Warsaw all night.

The Forum sounded prohibitively expensive, the Warszawa a trifle municipal. The Peasant's Home appealed to my streak of meanness, but it also had a primitive ring. 'Saski,' I announced briskly.

I met Pawel in a restaurant in the Royal Way after a morning spent admiring the Stalinist obelisks of the city centre. Warsaw is richer in these strange monuments than the other cities I had seen. Perhaps the Polish communists under Bierut wished to disprove any suggestion of disloyalty to Moscow by having more of them built in Warsaw than any other communist capital.

The richest example among this genre is the fanciful and eclectic Palace of Culture, which was not, however, built upon Polish initiative. It was a 'gift' from Stalin to the city of Warsaw, or rather a reminder to the people of Poland of where their priorities lay. Stalin was probably aware that he was continuing an old tradition of the Russian Tsars who habitually presented 'gifts' of huge orthodox cathedrals to the subject peoples of Finland and the Baltic.

The Palace of Culture has a strong resemblance to Moscow State University, with which it shares the appearance of a wedding cake. Like an outlandish pyramid, it dominates the surrounding city with its Egyptian or Assyrian-style colonnades topped by balconies surmounted with pineapples. And like an Pharoah's pyramid, the spirit of the age in which it was constructed now seems as distant and incomprehensible as some strange medieval sect.

Pawel was sitting in the restaurant opposite me. He was short, dark and slender. Most young Poles I had seen were large, blond and muscular. Pawel was a weedy little fellow, however, and I initially mistook him for a Turk. As I stumbled through the menu under the tired gaze of a bored waitress, he introduced himself in a very colloquial German.

'So you are German,' I said thankfully.

'No,' he answered, bristling immediately. 'I live in the DDR, but I am Polish. I am studying medicine in Leipzig.'

'How nice,' I said non-committally. It always seemed best to begin in that vein.

'It certainly isn't. I hate it.'

Pawel shared Opa's spleen for the DDR. But in Pawel's case, a cordial dislike had hardened into something much more vitriolic through the experience of daily life. We made a terrible combination. I had not lived long enough in East Germany to grow bored with confinement but had been just long enough to drink deep of a country which seemed to be almost too thoughtful for its own good. With my western passport, the Wall presented me with no terrors. It was the locked door behind which there was a room in which I could hear voices but into which I had never entered.

Pawel saw it from quite another angle. For him, it was the closed door which barred the way between Poland and its rightful communication with the west. It was wealthier than Poland, and therefore a subject of jealousy. But it was not nearly wealthy enough to have accumulated West Germany's glamorous reputation. The East German's humdrum prosperity had, moreover, been achieved through a strict adherence to classical socialism. In Polish eyes, such a prosperity was more offensive than remaining in the direst poverty, particularly as it suggested that the Poles could have achieved the same thing.

Pawel parried every positive statement I made about his adopted country with the formula, 'I've seen something quite different', or, 'That just isn't so.' I was still touched by my recent encounter with Dagmar and Baronius, stoically touring the gas ovens erected by their parents and grandparents, but Pavel waved his hand to remonstrate against any suggestion of East German humility. 'I'm sorry,' he said severely, 'but the East Germans are the most racist people in the entire world. They are far worse than the West Germans.' I felt that for all their lack of opportunities to travel abroad, the

East Germans were remarkably open-minded, perhaps on account of having watched so much television in the same language but from either side of the great European divide. 'I've seen something very different,' said Pawel. 'In fact the East Germans are particularly *narrow*-minded. They're afraid of their own government and of us Poles and what we may get up to.' There was no pleasing Pawel on the issue. I made the mistake of assuring him that by the time he had finished his studies he would surely have made many German friends, upon which he shot me a look of such startling dislike that I thought we had better drop the subject entirely.

It was quite clear from the start that Pawel and I disliked each other intensely. But he was on holiday in Warsaw and so was I and like one of those dismal couples who cling to one another out of a desperate fear of what might happen if either was to be left alone, neither of us had the will power to cut the Gordian knot and go our separate ways.

We rattled and snapped our way round Warsaw together, grating on each other's tenderest sensibilities and inwardly screaming with jangled nerves. To fill up the gaping silences, we ate an extraordinary amount of food. We ate schnitzls and salads for lunch in a café in the Royal Way. We ploughed angrily through icecream and cakes in the Hotel Victoria. We knocked down aperitifs in the Hotel Europejska. Finally we waddled up to the Old Town to cram a couple of steaks into our bulging bellies.

So much meat was not a good idea as the fizzing and popping of the acids in our stomachs made us more splenetic and irascible than ever. 'I tell you, we Poles are never free,' Pawel told me as he wiped away the grease that was dribbling down his cheeks from the final dreary feast of the day. 'Ugh,' I grunted between scrunches and slurps, before beginning my own private tirade about the insolent carriage of the waiter. Pawel's remark appeared so ridiculous, more fitting for the barricades than a fancy restaurant, cramming down steak and cream caramel with flagons of wine.

From the vantage point of Warsaw, the café life I had once enjoyed in the middle European cities of Berlin and Prague appeared as mournfully distant as the roar of a retreating tide. Shadows of former elegance exist only in a caricatured form in the internationalised setting of the big hotels, where it is wholly divorced from the world outside.

I became more aware than ever in Warsaw of how many stairs I had bumped my way down since leaving Berlin and how many bruises I had sustained in the descent.

Many people in the west have a glamorised view of Poland on account of the majestic drama of the church's historic confrontation with the forces of an atheistic and unpopular state. Poland is plucky – full of spunk. It is a place in which journalists can dwell on the paradox of religious faith under communism. They have seen pictures of the pope and of Lech Wałesa leading great demonstrations against the government and assume the Poles have achieved something that their neighbours have not. But from the point of view of the traveller who has come from Berlin, rather than from London or Washington, the impression is different. It seemed to me that the reasons for the continual protests of the Poles lay not so much in some unique personal characteristic as in the uniquely shambolic character of the Polish economy, which is unable to deliver even the most basic facilities to its citizens. The Poles are still in chains, but unlike the Czechs, the chains are not 'made of sausages'.

Warsaw on a dull day seems a caricature of a child's guide to eastern Europe. Here a vista of run-down tower blocks. There the odd temple dedicated to Stalin's 'ghastly good taste'. There was nothing to retreat into and nowhere to relax. I moved out from two-star hotel into a four-star hotel and found that if anything it was still worse. Only the bill had changed. The water was still not hot, the restaurant was still a sulphurous cavern serving cold schnitzls in an oily mess. The waiters startled me by creeping up behind my table without my notice and whispering 'Dollars?' in my earhole. Raggedy-anne tarts still plied their trade from the corner tables of the café, announcing without any finesse, 'Hello. Yes, you. Come here,' to anyone sitting within a radius of twenty feet. I found no oasis into which I could withdraw, lick my wounds and emerge triumphant the following day, refreshed and invigorated enough to withstand another dose of daily life in Poland.

In the bars of the international hotels the foreign businessmen sat in squelchy leatherette armchairs spaced several yards apart, shouting at one another and ogling the prostitutes.

Pawel was quite puzzled when I suggested we track down a few old-fashioned cafés and bars to find a little more authentic atmosphere.

'How about the Hotel Victoria?' he said. 'It's the best place in Warsaw.'

'The *Victoria*!' I exploded. 'For God's sake, Pawel, that place is as atmospheric as an airport lounge!'

'The Victoria is the best,' he said stubbornly, and as I sensed another storm brewing, I agreed to go along.

The bar at the Victoria looked exactly like an airport lounge and all that was missing was an intercom accouncing the time of the next flight to Kuala Lumpur. The clientele was strictly airport lounge as well. The Victoria is also the main vcnue for the Warsaw 'girls' I had been told about in the Polish tourist office.

The 'girls' in the Hotel Victoria were very thin. I was struck by this quality as their counterparts in my hotel were uniformly fat. One explanation for this phenomenon is that my hotel was almost entirely patronised by Middle Eastern businessmen, who have a reputation for liking plump women.

The clientele at the Hotel Victoria, on the other hand, was almost entirely Scandinavian, German or British, people who do not generally esteem excessive curves. The girls also appeared to work in a kind of team, as there were several stationed at strategic points around the bar and outside the door. They wore the same thigh-high red skirts and tiny clutch bags. Sometimes they crossed the floor to chat briefly with one another and swap cigarettes. There was much exchange of whispered confidences with the bar staff.

'Hello,' the first one murmured as we sallied into the bar. Pawel sat down in one of the giant leatherette armchairs which grunted responsibly.

'What a great bar!' said Pawel contentedly.

'Very nice,' I agreed.

'Hello,' said the girl again. We were not very far away from her.

'Those girls speak four or five languages each,' said Pawel, adopting a scientific tone. 'They are all proficient in English, French, German and Russian.' Business was brisk that evening in the Hotel Victoria. The small tables which lined the window were all occupied by single businessmen, who idly fingered the stems of their wine glasses and passed hopeful, loaded glances at the girls standing nonchalantly around the bar. Occasionally one would summon up the courage to get up, walk with studied casualness across the floor and talk to one of the girls. At one point, three men got up simultaneously and had to queue politely behind one another to talk to the same girl. They did not look the least embarrassed about this, however. The first one coughed slightly and then inclined his head to whisper something in her ear. The girl cocked her head on one side to think about it for a little, before wiping the cracked smile off the face of her potential client with a short sharp shake of her head. No deal. Here, he lost his nerve, for the entire room was now watching him intently. Instead of returning to finish his drink, he scuttled quickly towards the exit and escaped. The second man now tried his luck. The tension in the bar was by this time unmistakable. It was as if no one could relax into their former conversations until the crisis had passed.

This time the girl quickly nodded, however. Without even acknowledging the third handsome prince waiting to say his piece, she knocked down her Pepsi in a single gulp and sailed out of the door. We all sighed with relief.

Pawel claimed to be acquainted with one of the ladies who 'worked' the Hotel Victoria although she was not there that night. 'She is a highly qualified psychiatrist,' he said. 'Her only motives are an interest in the human mind.'

Behind our chairs sat four English businessmen. They were well dressed and spoke with Cockney accents.

'Two hundred dollars,' one of them began. I mentally checked this with the figure given by the tourist office and found it correct.

'... I think she was called Catherine, no not that one over there, Katrina maybe. 'Course I asked to her show her tits and she flopped them right out, weighed a ton each one ...'

I relayed this conversation for Pawel's benefit without any comment at all, but Pawel now rounded on me with all the pent-up fury that had been building up throughout our long, bilious day.

'Why did you translate that conversation for me?' he asked angrily.

'I just thought you might be interested,' I snapped back.

'You are a *snob*,' Pawel nearly shouted. 'A Goddamned English *snob*.'

'What is so snobbish about telling you that conversation?' I demanded.

'The conversation was irrelevant. You are a snob because every

133

Englishman is a snob.' As this was the second time I had heard this comment I felt irritated. I felt particularly irritated because there seemed no way of arguing back against a characteristic that had been attributed regardless of any personal qualities to an entire nation. I am, therefore I am a snob, seemed to be the gist of it.

I got up and hurriedly put on my coat, determined to make a dignified end of it. Some curious sense of honour made Pawel stand up and solemnly announce, 'Here is my card.' I was so surprised by the gesture that my anger was caught off guard. Without saying another word, I placed it in my wallet and left.

WARSAW

Old Town

'What the Poles are doing for us is a blessing . . . .
Warsaw will disappear, Warsaw the capital of sixteen
or seventeen million Poles, a people who blocked the
east to us for seven hundred years . . . will be no more.'

Himmler to Hitler, on the Warsaw uprising of 1944

IN THE HEART of Bierut's reconstructed Warsaw are the clustered
red roofs and baroque façades of the Old City and the Royal Way.
They seem as incongruous as a country cottage next to a supermarket,
but the 'old town' of Warsaw is really as much a part of modern
Warsaw as the Palace of Culture and the Hotel Forum. For in 1944
the entire city of Warsaw was razed to the ground on Hitler's orders
as a punishment, following the Warsaw uprising of August 1944.

The rebellion was a disastrous miscalculation. In the summer of
1944 the Russian armies were advancing at great speed through Byelorussia and the eastern marches of pre-war Poland towards Warsaw.
In July it was noticed that there was an air of panic among some
of the German personnel in the city. The Poles wished to liberate
themselves rather than be liberated by the old Russian enemy, and
in the expectation of a rapid German collapse a disorganised revolt
broke out against the Germans on 1 August 1944.

Instead of liberation there came destruction. Stalin had no intention
of allowing the Poles to be free of German armies unless it was on
condition of their being supplanted by his own. He left the desperate

rebels of Warsaw to fight a furious but useless battle against the vengeful German forces. Not only that, he refused to allow Allied airplanes to use Russian airfields, from which supplies could have been delivered to the rebels, until the revolt was nearly crushed. Hitler was delighted by the opportunity to destroy the remainder of the city. Two hundred thousand Poles were killed in the fighting and at least three quarters of a million more were deported. The liberated Warsaw of January 1945 consisted principally of rubble.

The city which Hitler pledged to raze to the ground, the citizens of post-war Poland pledged to rebuild. It was one of the few things that bound the aspirations of the ordinary Poles to those of their new Russophile government. The Old Town which delights the tourists of today with its picturesque charm is entirely a reconstruction made with the aid of old photographs and the memories of former inhabitants.

The Warsaw ghetto, however, was not rebuilt in the same manner as the adjacent Old Town, perhaps because the vast majority of its inhabitants perished during the deportations to concentration camps and the final destruction of the ghetto by the Nazis in 1943.

The tourist authorities seemed almost embarrassed by the memory of the Jewish ghetto. My bus tour of the city hurtled through the district and only stopped to let us out to see the memorial to the victims of the ghetto when a Jewish-American couple loudly protested that this had been the only object of their visit to Warsaw. The monument, erected in 1984, was designed to resemble the 'Wailing Wall' in Jerusalem. The block of stone from which it is carved was originally brought to Warsaw to serve as the base of a statue of Hitler.

Warsaw was once the largest Jewish city in Europe. In the entire world it was second only to New York. In 1938 almost one third of the population of Warsaw was of Jewish extraction. In the autumn of 1939, Warsaw fell victim to the Nazi invaders. The Jewish citizenry was immediately subjected to the usual haphazard persecutions. It was not until November 1940, however, that the Nazis erected a wall around the area of the ghetto within which all Jewish citizens were confined. From 15 November the high walls and barbed-wire fences were patrolled by German and Polish policemen to prevent the Jews from leaving the precincts. Small boys nicknamed 'catchers' continued to risk certain death by crawling under the barbed wire into the 'aryan' side of the city to make forays for food on behalf of their slowly starving families.

With that unmerciful discipline and sense of order that characterised the Nazi occupation everywhere, the Nazis insisted on the formation of a responsible Jewish city government, the 'Judenrat', whose duty it was to govern the Jewish community until the time when the Nazis had the opportunity to exterminate them. Upon these luckless citizens fell the responsibility of authorising the Nazi decrees in the ghetto, including the almost daily death sentences and the deportations to the death camps. The Germans regularly entered the ghetto and slaughtered civilians who happened to be on the street. Once it was a pregnant woman who had slipped over and caught the soldier's eye. Another time it was a child sitting outside the Jewish hospital waiting to be treated. For some of the German soldiers a popular form of entertainment was to lie in wait in civilian clothes by the tiny holes from which the Jewish children crawled to find food and shoot them like rabbits as they emerged. In July 1942 the German authorities made the Judenrat responsible for the most savage decree of all, namely the deportation of the majority of the ghetto's 300,000 or so inhabitants to the concentration camps where they faced certain death. As an inducement, rations of bread and marmalade were offered to those who voluntarily agreed to 'deportation'. It was well known, however, what fate awaited those who accepted this bait and the chairman of the council committed suicide rather than sign the decree. From September 1942 only about 60,000 Jews remained in Warsaw. It was this rump of the Jewish population which staged a revolt between 19 April and 3 May 1943 which gave Hitler the excuse for destroying the rest of the Jewish community. Many children attempted to escape through the sewers, but most were hunted and destroyed like vermin. By 10 May 1943 the ghetto was destroyed.

The reconstructed old city divides neatly into three parts; a long gracious avenue known as the Royal Way; the Old Town and the New Town.

The Royal Way is lined with pastel-coloured shops, hotels, churches and statues of Polish 'alumni'. One of the most delightful, because it is so unexpected, is at number 35. It is named 'A. Blickle' and is a first-class pastry and confectionery shop, founded in 1869 and decorated with many photographs of the Blickle family.

A little further towards the Old Town is the church of the Holy Cross, built in 1682 and consecrated by Cardinal Radzielowski in the presence of Queen Maria Kazimiera. The baroque design of the church was modelled on the church of St Andrea della Valle in Rome. There is a marble epitaph to Frederick Chopin containing the composer's heart. A few doors down the street another plaque commemorates the house where the composer lived with his parents. In the church of the Holy Spirit was crowned Stanisław August, the last king of Poland.

King Stanisław, like Princess Victoria of Prussia, was a monarch who was cheated by fate of the opportunity 'to do good'. He acceded to the throne of Poland in 1764 with Russian support. His patrons naturally expected him to be a useful cipher who would do nothing to arrest the century-long slide of this sprawling empire into political decadence and military weakness. Much to their surprise and alarm he promptly set about ensuring Poland's future independence through enlightened reforms of its anarchic, aristocratic system of government.

The elective throne of Poland and the system of 'liberum veto' by which any single member of the Polish Diet could block the passage of legislation attracted the praise of European philosophers in the seventeenth century for the checks they made upon the ambitions of potential tyrants. A century later, however, the growth of powerful centralised monarchies in the surrounding states of Russia, Austria and Prussia had made the endless quibbling of the Polish parliament an insupportable luxury.

King Stanisław raced against time to gather in the harvest whilst the stormclouds gathered overhead. Putting aside the interests of his family, he converted the elective throne of Poland, always a fertile source of intrigue, weakness and foreign intervention, into a hereditary monarchy vested in the House of Saxony. The universities were prised out of the grip of the church and placed under the reforming hand of a state department of education. Taxes were reorganised. Many peasants were freed from serfdom, for the king realised that their pitiable servitude under the Polish aristocracy made them indifferent to the question of national independence. The king had drunk deep from the well of the eighteenth-century enlightenment. He encouraged the spread of the ideas of Rousseau and Edmund Burke at the Polish court. He noted the establishment of the constitution of the United States of America with particular interest and determined on providing his backward country with the same benefits.

These magnificent efforts came to nothing. The feckless Polish aristocracy had squandered the preceding century in the struggle to maintain every jot and tittle of their privileges. Russia, Austria, and the kingdom of Prussia were appalled by the prospect of a reformed and reinvigorated Poland, just when it seemed about to fall into their grasp like a ripe plum. That phoney old 'enlightener', the Empress Catherine of Russia, was particularly outraged by the spectacle of this piffling monarch actually achieving what she, for years, had only talked about.

Messages passed between Berlin, St Petersburg and Vienna. Then they struck in 1772, dividing the provinces of Galicia, West Prussia and Byelorussia between them.

Like one of those people who simply refuse to die even when several of their limbs have been amputated, Stanisław busily continued with his reforms. On 3 May 1791 they found their embodiment in the new Polish constitution, the first of its kind in Europe.

It was a triumph of royal reason over ecclesiastical obscurantism and aristocratic privilege. How different would the future not only of Poland but all of eastern Europe have been if this constitution had been allowed to put down roots and spread its branches over the less fortunate citizens of East Prussia and Russia. Out from the Diet went the phalanx of backwoods nobles who had stymied progress in the past. Along with them went their precious 'liberum veto'. In came a host of representatives from the newly enfranchised towns.

Far away in St Petersburg, surrounded by the craven popinjays of her court, the patience of the Empress of Russia finally snapped. There was a further flurry of letters between St Petersburg, Berlin and Vienna. In her design to destroy Poland once and for all, the empress secured the help of those old malingerers in the body politic, the Polish aristocracy. A body of them signed a treacherous treaty, the Confederation of Targowice, with the empress in St Petersburg. In response to their invitation, the Russian armies invaded in 1793 and virtually wiped Poland off the map. The Third Partition was a mopping-up exercise. Poor Stanisław August left for enforced exile in St Petersburg.

None of the statues along the Royal Way commemorate any of the architects of the modern Polish state as it has arisen since the Second World War. One is of Bierut's old foe, Cardinal Wyszinsky, the redoubtable Polish primate. Another is to the nineteenth-century poet, Adam Mickiewicz, who was born in Lithuania.

There is, in fact, scarcely any mention of the Polish path to socialism in any public monument in Warsaw. The Yugoslavs have their statues of Josip Tito. The passive Czechs have endured a museum to Klement Gottwald. The streets of East Berlin are criss-crossed with the names of Zetkin, Grotewohl and Luxemburg. In Warsaw the public era since the Liberation of 1945 has simply been passed over.

Adam Mickiewicz was a revolutionary, though of a romantic, Christian and nationalist kind. He was born in 1798 in the city of Vilnius. At the time, the cultures of Poland and Lithuania had been tightly interwoven by the union of the two states into the Polish Commonwealth. Like many Poles, Mickiewicz looked upon Lithuania as much as Poland as his home. In 1834 he wrote in a poem from Paris: 'Lithuania, fatherland of mine. You are like vitality. An outcast now in foreign climes. I see you in all your glory.'

In 1824 he was deported from Russia for founding a secret Polish society and from then on he moved round Europe like an *episcopus vagans* of revolution, blessing and encouraging not merely Poles but all oppressed nationalities, including Jews, to rise against their pygmy-like oppressors. Leavened by his socialist and Christian convictions, however, Michiewicz disdained the narrow nationalism which sought to replace one racial dominance by another, believing that the path to liberation also implied rising above the petty national hatred which the dismal despotisms of the Russians encouraged.

Although his country had recently been partitioned and the greater part absorbed by Tsarist Russia, Michiewicz had the closest of friendships with the Russian idealists who staged the futile liberal-minded revolt in St Petersburg in the December of 1830. He also greatly admired the Jews who neither then nor at any other stage in history have enjoyed much affection in Poland.

Mickiewicz has exercised an enduring fascination on the Polish intelligentsia. His name was bound up with the rebellion that broke out in both Poland and Lithuania in 1830. In the 1880s his thoughts impressed themselves onto the quick and receptive imagination of the young Rosa Luxemburg as she studied in the Russian Second Gymnasium for Girls in Warsaw. As recently as 1968, his play *The Forefathers* was banned from the stage on account of the dangerous emotions it was stirring amongst the predominantly student audience.

At the top of the Royal Way the road opens out into the broad square of the Royal Castle, from which one enters the narrow lanes of the Old City. In the middle of the square there is a tall column, upon which stands the effigy of King Sigismund III, who remodelled the adjacent castle into Swedish baroque style. The castle was the site of the Polish parliament from the sixteenth century to the time of the eighteenth-century partitions.

The cathedral of St John, a gothic structure dating from the four-teenth century, is the oldest church in Warsaw. As it was destroyed in 1944 and was subsequently rebuilt, it does not have the same architectural interest as the cathedral in Crakow, nor is there anything in it to compare with Crakow's royal tombs. There are several graves of interest, however, such as those of the last Masovian dukes from the 1520s, and that of the first president of independent Poland, Gabriel Nartowicz.

The tale of the short presidency of Mr Nartowicz is an illustration of the fragile instability of the new Polish state that was reconstituted in 1918, for his period in office lasted precisely two days. As a candidate of the centre and the left, his inauguration roused the full fury of the conservatives, many of whom attributed his electoral success to the machinations of the Jews. After two days of rioting he was assassinated on 16 December 1922.

Underneath the church there is a large crypt, built like a maze with many tiny corridors that open into small halls. Here lie the tombs of the archbishops of Warsaw and primates of Poland. The tomb of the most important of these archbishops has now been elevated into the body of the church where it has been installed in a chapel of its own. It belongs to Cardinal Archbishop Stefan Wyszinsky, over whose massive stone grave hangs a shield embellished with the words 'Polonia Semper Fidelis'.

This granite-faced man had no counterpart in the secularised societies of England or America in the twentieth century. One has to look back to Cardinal Manning or still further to St Thomas à Becket to find an English ecclesiatic of comparable stature. Wyszinsky was, to use the Ottoman term, a 'Basha Millet', the ecclesiastical leader of his nation. The circumstances that allowed Cardinal Wyszinsky to exercise such a crucial role in Polish society were similar in some basic respects to those which had elevated the English saint.

In Poland, as in the England of King Henry II, the forces of church and state collided as armies of equal strength, each with its own generals who presided over a determined and disciplined hierarchy. Beckets and Wyszinskys do not appear in societies like the Russia of the 1920s or the Albania of the 1960s, where the government is ruthlessly determined to uproot and extirpate the influence of religion. In Poland the communist authorities dared do no more than curtail the church's privileges, by removing it from the sphere of education and nationalising the church lands.

Divested of the responsibility of power, but with its prestige and personnel intact, the church was well placed to play the role of the nation's spiritual overlord. At only one point did the state show signs of wishing to break this tacit division of spheres of influence, at the height of the Cold War in the early 1950s. On trumped-up charges of spying and so forth, several bishops were arrested and the Cardinal Archbishop was forcibly retired to a monastery. The sentences were mild, however, compared with the relentless assault on the life of the church in Russia, post-war Hungary and Czechoslovakia.

Beside the tomb of Cardinal Wyszinsky I watched one elderly working-class man and his poorly dressed wife pay their respects. The old man started to weep and had to be dragged away from the stone slab by his wife. The reverence which the church and its clergy enjoy among a large section of Polish society are in some ways an indication of the unhealthy condition of Polish society and the economy. In Warsaw and Crakow one cannot avoid noticing the large number of educated and intelligent-looking young men who have donned black cassocks. In a western country the greater part of them would be involved in economics, business or scientific research. In Poland, as in seventeenth-century Spain, it is the church which draws on the aspirations of a great proportion of the nation's educated youth, to the detriment of other spheres of life. The number has risen sharply since before the war.

The centre of the Old Town is a large square, which is lined by tall burghers' houses. Many of these houses nearly fell down in the early years of this century when the middle classes decamped from the city centre to the suburbs. Fortunately in the 1930s it became fashionable again as a quarter for artists and architects.

One of these old houses now contains the Museum of the City of Warsaw. Beside it are several bars and cafés, where tourists and the better off citizenry congregate for the evening. In a cellar in the corner of the square is the Café Largactil, a fashionable meeting place for young people which made a reputation for itself by specialising in iced cakes made in the shape of women's breasts with cherries on top. Perhaps some local feminists raised objections, because they were no longer on sale when I visited. Almost next door is a Hortex café and restaurant. Hortex establishments are to be found in most Polish cities and enjoy a high reputation with some visitors on account of the quality of their icecreams, cakes and coffees. I have never understood why, though perhaps I always chose the wrong items. At any rate, the interior of the Hortex in Warsaw's Old Town Square is every bit as dreary and slovenly as most of the other cafés in Poland and the service was just as appalling.

The area of the reconstructed old city includes not only the Old Town, but also the adjacent New Town on the other side of the city wall. To reach the New Town one passes through the city wall via the Barbican, built in the mid-seventeenth century by Giovanni Baptista. In the summer the Barbican is the haunt of students and hippies selling bangles and strumming on guitars. A great deal more money seems to be made from begging off the tourists who pass through the narrow arch than from selling bangles.

The churches of St John and St Jacek on either side of the street signal one's arrival in the New Town. A plaque marks the house in which Marie Curie was born and which is now a museum.

The centre of the New Town is a comfortably sized square which is dominated by a whitewashed baroque church dedicated to St Kazimier. The church dates from the 1680s and is in the shape of a Greek cross. The Greek flavour is accentuated by the dazzlingly white interior, relieved only by an epitaph to Marie Caroline, wife of King John III, and a tableau opposite which depicts the destruction of the church in 1944. When I visited there was an exhibition of fine seventeenth-century chasubles.

The Café Bomboniera on the corner of the square was the only such establishment in Warsaw which evoked in me any kind of enthusiasm. It was neither pitch dark, nor illuminated with red light bulbs, nor was there loud pop music. I ate an excellent cheesecake. My pleasure was only dulled when the waitress roundly cursed me for leaving my camera behind for approximately thirty seconds and not paying her a tip for returning it to me when I came back to collect it.

BALTIC

Vilnius

ON MY LAST evening in Warsaw I examined the sheaf of documents which had been sent to me in Prague by Intourist Moscow Ltd. These authorised me to make the journey to Leningrad via Vilnius and Riga. I was due to cross the border between Poland and the Soviet Union at Grodno.

I viewed the border crossing at Grodno with some gloom as I felt that I would be parting from a society which for all its recent history was still perceptibly part of the western world with which I was familiar. The Cyrillic letters with which Grodno was marked on the map carried with them the overtones of a more alien culture. Had I made the journey from Berlin to Leningrad all at once, I should not have attached so much importance to the matter of the Cyrillic letters. But the slow pace of the journey, as I inched my way through eastern Europe towards Russia, made me sensitive to delicate changes in atmosphere and surroundings. One by one the cords that bound me to the west were snapping.

Buying a train ticket from Warsaw to the USSR in advance from the Polish travel office in London seemed a brilliant idea at the time. This privilege cost a great deal extra than the normal price, however. I was surprised, upon reporting to the Hotel Forum on Friday evening four hours before the departure of my train, to find that the hotel authorities had never heard of either my ticket, or, so it appeared, of the Polish travel office in London.

'Why don't you call in at their offices in Warsaw?' one of the hotel officials suggested. I asked when it would next be open.

'Monday.'

'Today is Friday. I have reserved a hotel in Vilnius for Saturday.'

The hotel assistant shrugged. 'If I were you I would cancel your holiday in the USSR and go back to London. When you get home you could always ask Intourist for your money back,' she said.

Warsaw Central Station at seven o'clock in the evening was in a state of Babylonish confusion. There are 40 million people in Poland and they are all breeding incredibly fast, if Opa's flat in Cracow and the number of babies I saw in the streets are anything to go by. A large percentage of this 40 million people seem to hang around in stations. This was my theory to explain why Polish railway stations were such a nightmare of people shouting, shoving and staggering around dead drunk. There is nothing illogical about hanging around in the station. If I was Polish, I would too. They are often the jolliest place in town in terms of entertainment, the number of cafés and warmth.

I was unable to speak enough Polish even to find the counter where they were selling tickets for Russia and was seriously considering taking the hotel assistant's advice and returning to London when a finger poked me in the back.

The finger belonged to a young African student with a charming, untrustworthy smile who was dragging behind him a train of suitcases that looked as if they could have kept half a dozen of the most fastidious travellers in clean clothes for a month. He spoke Russian, but upon realising that I was foreign, he switched happily into fluent French. He appeared quite delighted to hear that I was going to Vilnius, as he was travelling to Leningrad, where he was studying medicine.

'Are you leaving tonight?' he asked. I explained that I wished to leave that evening but that I had no ticket and had no idea how to buy one. The student smiled. 'No problem. We will get our tickets together.' We made our way through the throng of travellers to counter number fifteen. On the way he introduced himself as Akogo from Togo.

At counter fifteen, Akogo pushed his way to the front and began a heated discourse with the woman selling tickets. The woman was clearly reluctant to make a deal. I assumed it was because I was British because she kept pointing at me through the glass and shouting at Akogo.

After the exchange had ended she gave me one last look, shrugged her shoulders in the way I imagine Pontius Pilate washed his hands, and passed two tickets over the counter. I thrust a fistful of złotys at her and examined these precious documents.

'Why have I got two?' I asked Akogo as we left the counter. 'I have a ticket to Vilnius and another to Leningrad.'

'The ticket to Leningrad is mine,' Akogo said sheepishly. 'I've run out of money.'

Akogo seemed to think I would be furious, and was surprised when I insisted on buying him supper in the restaurant of my hotel. The last supper in Warsaw.

The restaurant had been turned into a discotheque for the evening. The waiter came up and took our orders. The lights from the disco kept alternating colours, so that the waiter was bathed one moment in red and the next moment he was all green. 'Want to change some money?' he murmured softly in my ear (he was now all yellow) when he returned to serve our pork chops.

The music became more Romantic as the evening went on. The hard rock melted into Frank Sinatra singing 'Strangers in the Night'. I forgot about Akogo and stared instead at the middle-aged couple sitting at the next table. The couple, who had also evidently been strangers to one another before the evening began, were courting furiously.

'Lovers at first sight,' the song continued, as the man lit up the woman's cigarette. She hesitated, then accepted, and in so doing looked him directly in the eye as if for the first time. 'No, no, please,' she said, without a great deal of conviction, as he poured her some more wine.

The room was almost dark, so that when the swing doors of the kitchen flew open and a waiter emerged, a white beam like a car headlamp shone on the dirty maroon carpet. In the kitchen one of the waiters was fondling the lady chef. She was still wearing her tall white chef's hat. In the split second before the door closed and plunged the room back into darkness, the chef's arm closed around the waiter's neck, a cigarette still held between her fingers.

Akogo and I went back to the station to wait for the Leningrad train. When it arrived we helped each other with our luggage, though it took some ingenuity to find the space to store away Akogo's various bits and pieces. 'Where on earth did you buy all this?' I asked as we panted into the carriage with the last load.

'Paris,' he answered. He had a worried expression on his face. 'I hope I don't have problems.' Akogo was reluctant to explain what these problems might be.

The curtains of the railway carriage were decorated with pictures of the battleship *Aurora*, from whose guns issued a beam bearing the legend '1917'.

Akogo and I were not alone in our compartment. A bucolic-looking Pole grinned cheerfully when we entered, a bottle of beer clasped in a huge hand. He was travelling to Leningrad to see his girlfriend, so he said. On the other side sat a well dressed young woman of about thirty. The Pole told us she was from Lithuania. Beside her sat a perfect-looking daughter in pig-tails. The woman from Lithuania looked up briefly at Akogo. Her face registered extreme distrust.

'What is your little girl's name?' Akogo asked her, parking himself beside her. She flinched.

'Gerda,' she replied gruffly.

'Does she speak English?' I asked.

'A little.'

'May I speak to her, then?' I continued.

'No.'

She got up and without another word hustled Gerda out into the corridor. Little Gerda was evidently going to be installed for the night in another, safer, compartment.

'I think she is afraid of you,' I teased Akogo, after the Lithuanian woman had disappeared into the corridor.

'They are often like that,' said Akogo philosophically, dismissing the subject. 'I can't wait till we are through the border. When we get through the border, they give you a nice cup of tea.'

The train started and soon we were dozing off on our bunks. I woke up once in the night to hear the train sound a mournful horn, like a whale looking for its mate.

The terrific jolt caused by the train stopping at the Soviet border nearly hurled me out of my bunk. Outside the window I made out the cyrillic letters 'Grodno'.

'Lithuania?' I enquired into the darkness.

'Byelorussia,' answered the Lithuanian woman underneath.

The door was flung open and by the light of a torch I had my first glimpse of Russia. It was a set of gold teeth.

'Passports,' said the gold teeth.

Akogo began to mumble softly. 'I hope I get through,' he said sadly. 'Once I'm through, I'll get my cup of tea.'

Akogo's obsession with getting over the Soviet border merely for the pleasure of a cup of tea mystified me. I lay on top of my bunk in the darkness, listening to the woman with gold teeth banging on the doors of the other compartments and demanding passports. From the darkness below, Akogo murmured: 'This is going to be frightful. They warned me Grodno was bad. I should have gone through Brest.'

The gold teeth, which I could now see belonged to a stout middle-aged lady, returned to our compartment. Her plump hand felt its way round the doorway and flipped on the light switch. She looked briefly at my passport and ignored me. Then she turned to Akogo.

'From Togo?'

He nodded.

'Luggage!' she said sharply. Akogo reluctantly got up from his bunk and taking as much time as possible, gingerly produced the first of his large suitcases from underneath his bed. The woman unzipped it, rummaged around and withdrew her hand. She was holding three women's make-up packages.

'Three!' she said accusingly. She rummaged around again and pulled out a plastic bag containing several dozen brightly coloured African scarves.

'Andrej!' she shouted ominously.

'Oh dear,' Akogo sighed heavily. 'I'm for it.'

I understood the significance of Akogo's cup of tea. The Pole and the Lithuanian woman did as well. The Pole sat on the edge of his upstairs bunk, frowning furiously, a huge pair of bare feet swinging from his bunk. The Lithuanian woman was up and looking as immaculate as the previous day in no time. She sat on her side of the bunk with a malicious smirk on her face, little Gerda planted on her lap. I suspected that she had brought Gerda in especially to watch the coming *auto de fé*.

'Andrej!' shouted the woman again. Another burly inspector entered the compartment and ordered Akogo to open all his belongings. One by one the suitcases emerged, from underneath his bunk, from underneath my bunk and from the luggage racks on top. All the suitcases were stacked up in the middle of the compartment and in another pile in the corridor. Each one was opened and the contents divulged. The Lithuanian woman, little Gerda, the Pole and I, were soon almost buried in silk scarves, bedspreads, jerseys, jeans and packets of ladies' make-up. In the middle of all this brightly coloured debris was Akogo.

'I knew Grodno was a mistake,' was the last thing he said, before he was removed from the train, along with Andrej, the woman with gold teeth and a mountain of brightly coloured scarves.

None of us went back to sleep after this incident and I, personally, felt it was indecent to accept the guard's offer of a cup of tea when Akogo was now marooned in Grodno station without his long-awaited cup.

At seven o'clock in the morning, the Pole produced a bottle of vodka, a large ham and a loaf of bread which he began to cut up with great enthusiasm.

'Cheers,' he said jovially, pouring me a vodka and clinking my glass, to the disapproval of the Lithuanian woman, who was now refashioning silent Gerda's perfect blonde pig-tails.

'Cheers,' said the Pole again, toasting the empty seat which had been occupied by our arrested colleague. It was early for drinking, but I felt the least I could do to honour Akogo's memory was to drink his health, so I took a vodka and clinked the Pole's glass. The Lithuanian woman looked on sourly. The Pole produced a large map, glanced at the No Smoking sign and lit up a cigarette. The Lithuanian woman tsked furiously and sent little Gerda back to the compartment where she had slept the night in safety. Not at all put off, the Pole poured another Vodka and placed a horny finger on the map where it was marked 'Vilnius'.

'Vilnius is Polish,' he announced. The Lithuanian woman shook her head vehemently. The Pole's horny finger moved southwards over the map and alighted over the Ukrainian city of Lvov.

'Lvov is also Polish,' he announced.

Quite unexpectedly, the Lithuanian woman burst out laughing. The noise came like a burst of gunfire, which broke the tension that had enveloped our compartment since the night before. Like two jackdaws, the two of them then began to chatter in rapid bursts of conversation. The Pole lit another cigarette with a satisfied smile (I suddenly imagined he was going to grab the Lithuanian woman by the shoulders and make love to her on the spot, with little Gerda right there, staring at them silently and immobile) and then they began to fire historical dates at each other. Each one was well armed with the relevant dates that proved Polish, Russian or Lithuanian ownership of the disputed cities Vilnius and Lvov.

The dawn gave way to a pale sunlit morning in which the Lithuanian countryside revealed itself by degrees through the mist. I expected some vast quantitative change in the appearance of the countryside now we were in the Soviet Union, and was curiously surprised to see that Soviet chickens and haystacks looked the same as those in Poland.

There was nothing to suggest we had crossed the border at all. There were tiny wooden cottages painted blue and red, with chickens in the farmyards, which reminded me of Poland. But the patchwork quilt of fields dotted with cornstooks and horses pulling ploughs had been displaced by bare rectagonal communal farms bordered with white tower blocks.

Poland had now become part of 'the west' in my mind, just as East Berlin had once been 'the west' when I crossed into Czechoslovakia. Upon deciding that Lithuania looked rather like Poland, I mentally crossed over another Berlin Wall. As always, I was both relieved and caught off balance by the discovery that each time I crossed this wall in my imagination it dissolved as soon as it was behind me.

A clutch of cream-coloured baroque spires told me we were in Vilnius. I dragged my suitcase out of the train, waved good bye to the Pole and stood in the square in front of the station. It was a reassuringly ordinary scene of trolleybuses, ladies carrying shopping bags and children on roller skates. 'No different from Poland,' I said to myself. Lithuania was already becoming 'the west' and once again

the wall shifted a couple of hundred miles eastwards to some unspeci-
fied point in between the Baltic states and Leningrad.

A blonde girl jumped out of a taxi. 'Oh Mr Tanner,' she said breathlessly, 'I only knew of your arrival a few minutes ago.' I failed to
understand how she knew of my arrival at all as there were several
trains daily from Warsaw to Vilnius and I could have arrived on
any of them. But I buried this disturbing difference between Vilnius
and Warsaw in the back of my mind and climbed gratefully into
the taxi.

The taxi drove us both to the Hotel Letuva. It was a smart, modern
establishment and a great improvement on the hotels I had seen in
Poland. In Poland, I often felt that travelling involved the worst elements of life in both east and west. I had the freedom to come and
go, but without any of the facilities that I expected would accompany
these freedoms. I had complete freedom of movement, but it seemed
like freedom to discover that there is no affordable hotel accommodation and freedom to wander the streets vainly searching for a café
where they served coffee with milk or a restaurant where there was
a choice of meals for the main course.

In the USSR, my movements were not free at all. All my hotel
and travel arrangements had to be prepared and approved in advance.
Once I had arrived, however, I felt that I had passed under the direct
observation of the Soviet government and that there were corres-
ponding advantages to go with this loss of freedom. At the Letuva
it was clear that my stay in Vilnius would be organised down to
the last detail and I felt curiously grateful to them for lifting the
burden of decision-making from my shoulders.

Seated behind the reception desk in a neat row were four girls.
They were all smiling broadly.

'Porter!' shouted one, and an old man grabbed my suitcase and
disappeared with it into the lift.

'Dinner?' asked the second and without waiting for an answer,
said, 'Yes. We will book a seat in the Senasys Rusys. This means
Old Cellar. It is a top class restaurant in the heart of the old town.
They serve Lithuanian specialities. The menu is in English, French,
German and Russian. You will like it.'

I was passed on to the third.

'Excursion?' I nodded. 'How many are there in your group?'

'One.'

'Grouph Number, One,' she wrote. She frowned as she wrote. 'One' is not a number the Soviet authorities feel comfortable with. 'You will have a tour of the city tomorrow at two o'clock with your own guide and chauffeur. That will be twenty-two pounds please.'

My guide was an attractive blonde with a taste both for English literature and parrying criticisms I had not made.

'Do you like Iris Murdoch?' she began. 'I expect you are surprised that her books are available in Vilnius. In fact you can buy them at the university bookshop. Iris Murdoch is very popular in Vilnius.'

Her habit of asking questions and supplying answers at the same time made our conversations rather difficult, as my replies had to include answers to the 'a' part of her statement and the 'b' part as well.

'Yes I do,' I replied to part 'a' of her question, 'and no I am not surprised,' I said, replying to part 'b'.

'I particularly enjoyed *A Severed Head*. Where are we now?'

The guide mentally inserted the cassette into her head which contained a learnt-by-rote speech which she had clearly delivered many hundred times before.

'We are in Gediminas Square. On the hill above the square is the castle. Its origin is as follows.

'There was a Grand Duke of Lithuania called Gediminas who fell asleep in the forest when he was out hunting. In his dream, he saw a giant wolf, howling on the top of a hill. An army of hunters were shooting arrows at the wolf, but their weapons bounced off the wolf's thick hide. In the morning the Grand Duke asked his most trusted wizard, a man named Lizdeika, to divine the significance of the dream about the wolf.

'The wizard told him the meaning of the dream. The wolf was the city of Vilnius, which Gedimins was to build on the nearby hill. The arrows bouncing off its hide showed that however many times the city would be besieged, it would never fall to the enemy. This is the legend of the origins of Vilnius.'

'It is a charming legend,' she mused, as she strode across the cathedral square. A flock of jackdaws arose from the wood that straggled behind the cathedral up the hill towards the castle and wheeled and cawed above her head.

'At present the cathedral is an art gallery, but we are thinking of returning it to the believers,' she added, parrying any potential objections about the conversion of the cathedral into a gallery. The cathedral was indeed returned to the catholic church shortly after I left Lithuania.

Vilnius cathedral is a severely classical church. The original construction in the 1380s was the first fruit of Prince Jogailia's conversion to Christianity. In the 1780s the cathedral was entirely rebuilt in a spirit of stern indifference to previous ecclesiastical tastes. The result is a fine building that would have made an excellent university senate, but it does not much look like a church. Its most interesting feature is the bell tower, which stands entirely separate from the cathedral in Gediminas Square.

The sixteenth-century church of St Kasimir is as exuberant and relaxed as the cathedral is severe and restrained. It is the oldest baroque church in Vilnius and the huge drum roof is topped by a royal crown, as the church's patron saint, St Kasimir, was the nephew of King Jogailo. The guide pointed to the rose-coloured rococo façade with embarrassment.

'There are twenty-two *functioning* churches in Vilnius,' said my guide heavily, ... 'but I'm afraid this one is the Museum of Atheism.'

'I suppose you think "Museum of Atheism" is a stupid title,' she said quickly.

'Well what do *you* think?' I responded.

'I am not a believer but I think it's a pretty stupid title. In this time of *glasnost* we are thinking of returning this church as well to the believers,' she said. 'Incidentally, who are ten most popular authors in England nowadays?'

Lithuania is a land of deep forests and sparsely populated marshlands. It was the least known corner of medieval Europe. The Lithuanians, alone amongst the Baltic nations, successfully resisted the *Drang nach Osten* of the Germans to the west. Armed with papal blessings for a crusade against the heathens, the German crusading orders moved eastwards to subjugate and annihilate the original Prussians. The fate of these Baltic Prussians remains a moot point of eastern European historiography.

These crusading orders, the Teutonic knights and the Livonian Order, conquered present-day Latvia and Estonia in the first half of the thirteenth century. The Lithuanians were now surrounded on two sides by the German settlers. To escape the fate that befell the Latvians, Estonians and Prussians, the Lithuanians united themselves into a kingdom, carved out a substantial empire for themselves in the lands to the east and south, and finally broke the ambitions of the Teutonic Knights at the battle of Grunewald in 1410.

The rise of Lithuania into a powerful European state in the fourteenth century was particularly remarkable, because Lithuanians were pagans. They clung to their old woodland gods and spirits many centuries after the rest of Europe had adopted Christianity, and only received the catholic faith as the price of an alliance with Poland in 1387.

Following the unification of the Lithuanian tribes in the 1230s under King Mindaugas, Lithuania followed the traditional pattern among new and endangered kingdoms by seeking the blessing of the Roman church through the adoption of christianity.

The normal course of such affairs would have involved the setting up of an ecclesiastical network of bishops and archbishops which would confirm royal as well as papal authority. But this course was broken in 1263, when King Mindaugas was murdered. Lithuania relapsed into paganism. This might have brought about the ruin of the kingdom, as any Christian prince could claim the sanction of a papal crusade against pagan neighbours. Instead there began the most glorious era in Lithuanian history.

In the early fourteenth century King Gediminas made his pagan kingdom into a large empire which stretched south and eastwards through the Ukraine towards Kiev. In spite of the power and size of the Lithuanian empire during this period, little is known of the religion practised by the fourteenth-century Lithuanians. As late as the early 1380s King Algirdas was buried in the old pagan rites, his body being burned on a funeral pyre with his brother, who had also recently died, and his hunting dogs. It was an agricultural religion which did not involve the construction of large temples. Instead, there were shrines situated in sacred groves set on hill tops. Here the Lithuanians worshipped a pantheon of small deities, of trees, rivers and bushes. The devil was often portrayed in the guise of a German. There may have been a strong belief in reincarnation or some form of after-life, as the Lithuanians had a reputation for committing suicide when they lost battles.

The Lithuanians might have continued the worship of nuts and bushes uninterrupted, had not the German danger made necessary the formation of a dynastic alliance with Catholic Poland. In 1386 King Jogailo married the young Queen Jadwiga of Poland in Cracow, so becoming ruler of both states. The joint rule of this large empire, King Jogailo decided, was worth a Mass. Lithuania officially abandoned its old gods and joined Christendom.

The Lublin Union of 1569 cemented this marriage of convenience by the formal proclamation of a Polish-Lithuanian commonwealth under a Lithuanian dynasty. The crowns of the Grand Duchy of Lithuania and the Kingdom of Poland were united in the same way that the crowns of England and Scotland were united under the Stuarts.

At first the two countries maintained a kind of parity, but after the death of Zygmunt Augustus, the last Lithuanian king of the commonwealth, in 1572, the more numerous Poles came to dominate the Lithuanians. The later kings of Poland neglected Vilnius. The age of the Polish-Lithuanian commonwealth permanently affected the architectural character of Vilnius, which began to resemble a provincial Polish city of small classical squares arcaded by the peaches-and-cream façades of baroque convents. From the Vilnius of old, only the Jewish quarter has entirely disappeared, owing to the Nazi occupation. Vilnius is no longer the 'little Jerusalem' it was in nineteenth-century Lithuania with its rabbinical seminary and great community of orthodox Jews. The area occupied by the Jews beside German Street, now Museum Street, was rebuilt after the Second World War.

With the partition of Poland in 1795, Lithuania became part of Tsarist Russia, but culturally the city of Vilnius remained largely Polish. This was the city which bore Adam Mickiewicz. Later in the nineteenth century, Vilnius nursed Rosa Luxemburg's companion in revolution, Leo Jogiches. Jogiches and Luxemburg together founded a left-wing branch of the Social Democratic party and owing to the strong links which still bound Lithuania and Poland they naturally named the party the 'Social Democracy of the Kingdom of Poland and Lithuania'.

After the outbreak of revolution in Russia in 1917 both Poland and Lithuania proclaimed their independence. The city of Vilnius was a bone of contention between them, but the *force majeure* of the Poles under Pilsudski enabled them to seize Vilnius again in 1920. In 1940 Vilnius became part of the new Soviet Republic of Lithuania, but even today a fifth of the population of Vilnius are of Polish descent.

Lithuania converted to Christianity when the age of gothic was almost at an end. Its present form is almost entirely shaped by the counter-reformation, whose architectural expression was the baroque form. The city contains one perfectly formed gothic church, however, which so captured the imagination of Napoleon when he stayed in Vilnius on the road to Moscow that he allegedly declared his wish 'to put St Anne's in my hand and take it back to Paris'. The church of St Anne is a nugget-sized jewel made entirely of red brick. It was built around 1501, by unknown architects. The red gothic ribs have been wrought with such fluidity and delicacy that it has the organic air of a building that has grown out of the soil.

The city contains one surviving gateway, known as the Dawn Gate. The street that leads up to the gate is the richest in relics of Vilnius's past. The burghers of Vilnius fought hard for permission from the Grand Dukes to build a wall and were only so allowed when the Tatar threat in the sixteenth century made any further delay perilous. The Dawn Gate is a white archway bearing the shield of the arms of Vilnius with its two griffons. Beside it hangs the head of Hermes, the symbol of the city's trading past. Beside the gate are the pink nougat-coloured walls of an orthodox monastery. On the other side is the baroque frivolity of the Basilian Gate, which leads to a former monastery that was closed under the tsars and converted into a political prison. The late eighteenth-century gate is embellished with strange symbols. They may be of masonic origin, as there were two freemasons' lodges in Vilnius in the eighteenth century.

It was only when I was some distance from the Dawn gate that I looked up and noticed the glass vestibule which projected from the first storey of the gateway over the street below. Inside I could see a small room containing a large icon set in a silver panel.

'The Madonna of the Dawn Gate,' said my guide, in a voice charged with a signal lack of enthusiasm. 'You can see it if you like. Just go through the door of the church on the left and climb the stairs up into the Dawn Gate.'

'Coming?'

'No. I will wait here.'

I entered the church by the side door and climbed the narrow staircase, nearly colliding with a rotund priest on the narrow, badly lit staircase as I went, before emerging at the end of a corridor into the sun-lit vestibule that housed the icon.

The dark icon was set into a beaten-silver panel indented with large hearts. Several elderly women were praying in front of the icon, assisted in their devotions by an old man in the corner who was pumping devotional tunes furiously on an organ. Down in the street I watched my guide flick open her make-up case to reapply some lipstick. She snapped the case shut when I descended.

'The Queen of Hearts,' I said gesturing to the icon. A few feet away in the street, a woman was kneeling on the pavement, her shopping bag beside her, eyes raised towards the icon above.

'Yes, it's very romantic,' admitted the guide. 'The icon resembles a seventeenth-century lady of Vilnius called Barabara Radrilaite. The Grand Duke of Lithuania, Sigismund August, fell in love with her, but she died very soon, poisoned, they say, by Queen Bonasforsza, the Duke's jealous mother.'

Queen Bonasforsza invited the Jesuits to Lithuania in the 1570s, and they exercised a preponderant influence in the Lithuania of the late sixteenth and seventeenth centuries. The Grand Duchy was the thin end of the catholic wedge surrounded by the hostile protestant powers of Prussia and Sweden to the west and orthodox tsarist Russia to the east. Vilnius was imprinted in the image of the counter-reformation with impressive baroque churches and convents as befitted the centre of catholicism in the Baltic region.

The Jesuits founded not only convents and monasteries, but a great university in Vilnius in 1579. The foundation of the university was an immense boon to the city. The university was expressly charged with the task of uprooting the ideas of the reformation amongst the educated classes, and with this in mind the Jesuits invited distinguished professors from all over Europe to Vilnius. The Jesuits also revived the literary use of the Lithuanian language in order to popularise their ideas amongst the poorer sections of society.

The heart of this great foundation was, as befitted a Jesuit university, a great baroque church, which was dedicated to St John. St John's was rebuilt in its present form in 1737, when the Jesuit era was drawing to a close. The last king of Poland expelled the Jesuit order from Poland in 1773 as part of the series of belated reforms designed to revive the fortunes of the Polish kingdom. The expulsion had immediate effect in Vilnius university, which became the property of the Polish state. After the partition of 1795, when Vilnius was absorbed into the Russia, the university inevitably became a hotbed of masonic, anti-Russian and revolutionary secret societies. It was closed by the Tsar in 1832 as a punishment for the part played by Lithuanians like Adam Mickiewicz in the uprising of the previous year. It was not reopened until 1919, following Lithuania's declaration of independence.

My guide accompanied me to the station to wait for the train for Riga. The sun was low and an autumnal chill had entered the air. 'How would you compare Vilnius to London?' she said as we sat on the station platform trying to catch the last of the sun's rays.

'There aren't very many cafés or restaurants.'

The guide was shocked by this statement. 'People from all over the Soviet Union say in Vilnius you cannot walk without falling over a café,' she remarked reprovingly.

Before the train came in I asked her opinions about Poland. I asked her about her feelings towards the nation whose fortunes had been linked with those of Lithuania for much of their joint histories, which had influenced the religious development of the country and shaped the physical form of the city of Vilnius.

She thought about this for a minute. 'I do not like the Poles,' she answered slowly, as if still trying to figure out why. The train to Riga suddenly appeared on the horizon and she stood up to help me with my luggage.

'Last year the Poles came in great numbers to Vilnius and bought all the television sets. People were saying you could hardly get on to the trains last summer, they were so full of Poles taking our television sets back to Warsaw.'

BALTIC

Riga

THE WIND BLEW up the streets of Riga in short gusts, whistling through the wooden eaves and pitched roofs of the port and mingling with the smells of cabbage and coffee wafting from the cafés and restaurants. The dusk was shedding its soft light in the streets. I could hear the sound of singing from Soviet sailors ashore for the evening as they stumbled across the cobbled alleys, arm in arm and hopelessly drunk.

I slumped down on to a park bench next to a stern-looking schoolgirl who was absorbed in an English textbook.

'I've been mugged,' I told her.

She looked up from her book. 'What is "mug"?'

'Hit, beaten. Two men held me by the arms against a wall as I came out of the hotel.'

'They must have been Russians.'

'They were Latvians.'

'Then they were trying to say hello or something.'

We both started laughing.

I was telling the truth. I had no sooner emerged from the front door of the Hotel Latvia than I was set upon by two young men who pinned me to the wall and made a rather feeble attempt to extract my wallet from my pocket. Although the Latvians are tall, well built people who sometimes made me feel that I was Gulliver in Brobdingnag, my two assailants were mercifully small and I was able to repulse them with ease. Still, it was unsettling and I wanted to tell someone all about it.

The girl on the park bench could not have been more than sixteen, but she had a look of fierce intelligence on her face that is common to central European schoolgirls. Her hair was pulled back sharply into a pony-tail, but the seriousness of her appearance was betrayed by the manner in which this auburn mass fell luxuriantly in waves down her back. The lips, though pursed, were full and wet.

'Your English is excellent,' I commented.

'I'm top of my class,' she said reproachfully, as if I should have guessed that to begin with.

'Let's go and sit in a café. I can tell you how I was mugged and you can tell me about Riga.'

'I don't believe you were "mugged,"' she said. 'And I never go to cafés. They waste time which could be spent in learning English or folk dancing.'

I imagined that Riga would continue in the same vein as Vilnius, though I knew that the Latvians had been more influenced by the Germans than their neighbours. I knew the Latvians were predominantly Lutheran in religion. But as I stepped off the train in Riga, I detected a quite different atmosphere from that of Vilnius.

Vilnius had a somewhat sleepy, provincial air. It was a city in which time lent itself ungrudgingly to hours spent gazing at the birds twittering as they gathered in the dusk on church spires.

Riga was bustling and Germanic, a city in which the fresh breezes from the Baltic make on reluctant to pause unnecessarily in one's business. The buildings are higher than those in Vilnius and the park in the centre of the city, with its pigeons, fat ducks and neatly edged flowerbeds, reminded me of London.

I felt as if my eastward journey from Berlin to Leningrad was taking me in a large circle, for Riga was steeped in the flavour of the old Germany of the eastern marches; of Brandenburg and East Prussia; of those restless medieval Germans' *Drang nach Osten*. The skyline was punctured with spires that might have come from Hamelin or Lübeck. Over them all soared the wooden spire of St Peter's church, which was topped with a golden cockerel. The streets of

Riga were lined with sturdy Hanseatic merchants' houses, many of them embellished with motifs declaring the year of construction and those rhyming couplets that were the hallmark of the pious and locquacious Germans of long ago.

The atmosphere was not only livelier than in Vilnius but also a great deal more tense. There were red flowers being laid on the Freedom Memorial outside my hotel. Amongst the flowers were letters and poems. In front of the memorial, youths wearing T-shirts with 'Riga calling' emblazoned on the front were stopping passers-by to collect signatures. One held a small banner on which was written 'Green Party'. A hundred or so people stood around arguing.

'How long has this demonstration being going on?' I asked my young girl friend.

'Months. They come here every morning with the flowers and don't go home until the night.'

'What are they talking about?'

'They are talking about Latvia.'

'That is a big subject, "Latvia!"'

'Formerly people were not allowed to put flowers on the Freedom Memorial. Now they are and they want to talk about everything. Some are talking about pollution. The letters and poems beside the flowers are calling for the release of political prisoners. Others are talking about whether the bourgeois republic was better than the Soviet republic. Between 1919 and 1940, you know, Latvia was a bourgeois republic.'

I asked her opinions about the bourgeois republic and she looked at me sharply. 'Do you work for the *Morning Star*? We read *Morning Star* and *Moscow News* in our English lessons.'

I assured her that I worked for neither the *Morning Star* nor *Moscow News*.

'In that case, I think the bourgeois republic was better than the Soviet republic. My grandfather was one of those who were deported when the Russians arrived in 1940. They said he was a "bourgeois nationalist". He didn't come back for twenty years.'

The Latvians have always been the pawns of powers greater than themselves and their history consists largely of being shuttled between Germans, Poles, Swedes and Russians with only the briefest of breathing spaces between the First and Second World Wars, when the great powers were too exhausted to do anything but let the Latvians in peace. Until 1940, when the whole sorry process began anew.

In the thirteenth century the German conquerors of Prussia received the blessing of Pope Innocent III to subdue the pagan Balts. In 1201 Bishop Albert conducted a small flotilla of German ships up the banks of the Daugava and erected what was to become the great Hanseatic port of Riga.

In 1220 a military crusading order known as the Knights of the Sword was established to secure German rule over the area around Riga. The Teutonic Knights failed to subjugate the neighbouring Lithuanians but by 1227 the conquest of present-day Latvia and Estonia was complete. In 1237 the Knights of the Sword were joined with the Teutonic Knights to rule what became called 'Livonia'.

According to legend, Bishop Albert captured Riga by duping the local Latvians into believing that his fort would be no bigger than an ox hide. The wily bishop then cut the hide into strips and stretched them around what is today the wall of the old city. It is not a very unusual legend, for there exists an identical tale from Ireland, but it illustrates Bishop Albert's enduring hold on the imagination of Riga's citizens.

There are a dozen tales of this energetic prelate. It is said that the bishop invented the symbol of the city, a golden cockerel, in a dream. Like most Latvian folk tales about the Germans, the sequel to the story is not flattering. Albert erected his golden cockerel on top of the spire of St Peter's, the magnificent church overlooking the harbour, where a replica remains to this day. The original cockerel apparently fell off, however, and smashed into a thousand pieces, in response to the prayers of the poor.

The conquest of Prussia by the Teutonic Knights spelled the eventual annihilation or absorbtion of the native Prussians, who left behind them only the name they donated to their new masters. In Latvia, although the urban settlements were wholly dominated by Germans, the native Latvians remained enserfed but otherwise undisturbed in the countryside.

The absolute domination of the Germans over Latvia was broken in the Livonian wars in 1550. But a brief twenty years of freedom, a prelude to the equally brief period of independence this century, gave way to the rule of a succession of foreign masters; Riga became part of the Polish-Lithuanian commonwealth from 1581 to 1621 before passing under Swedish rule from 1621 to 1710; from 1710 until 1917 it was part of Tsarist Russia.

The Swedish 'imperium' is commemorated by a stained-glass window in Riga cathedral in which the city fathers are reluctantly handing over the keys of the city to a resplendent and silver-clad Gustavus Adolphus. The German *burgermeisters* of Riga had some sound economic reasons to be gloomy. Gustavus Adolphus and Charles XII were accustomed to rule over a free peasantry as in Sweden and they both attempted, without much success, to mitigate the hardships faced by the native Latvian serfs at the hands of the German landowners.

The city's only surviving gateway at the end of Brewer Street is still called the 'Zviedru Varti' or Swedish Gate. Its stones apparently still harbour the walled-up corpse of an unfortunate Latvian maiden who was caught attempting to elope with her Swedish lover.

The vigorous and reforming hand of Sweden was displaced by the dead hand of Tsarist Russia at the beginning of the eighteenth century. After Peter the Great's historic victory over Charles 11 of Sweden at the battle of Poltava, the city of Riga fell to the Russians in 1710. The Tsar was eager to begin the bombardment of the city himself, as he had been coldly received in Riga thirteen years previously whilst visiting on an embassy. The Tsar personally fired the first three shells into the city and wrote afterwards, 'Thus the Lord God has enabled us to begin our revenge on this accursed place.'

In spite of these blood-curdling lines, Peter and his successors left Riga under the control of the German merchant community. The Germans continued to dominate the city council of Riga until the first decade of the twentieth century, in an ascendancy comparable to that of the Anglo-Irish in Dublin, thanks to the patronage they enjoyed from the tsars.

Although the tsars were happy for the Germans to run Riga, many of the native Latvians were not. A bronze cat opposite the State Philharmonia attests to the irritation felt by one Latvian at the Germans' exclusivity. It was erected by an angry Latvian merchant on top of his house in Horse Street, with its bottom facing towards the entrance into the guildhall opposite and to which he had been refused admittance. A copy of the cat still stands there, though its posterior now points the other way.

There are many other tales of the *kleinburgerlich* snobbery of the Baltic Germans. The city's streets were then so narrow that neighbours could shake hands through the overhanging windows on opposite sides of the street. In one such street two German merchants' wives were approaching from different directions. When they met, the width of their voluminous dresses did not allow more than one to pass at any one time. But who should give way? Both insisted that the poorer must give way to the richer, but agreement could not be reached on whose husband was the more prosperous, and so they remained where they were.

The Germans have now departed from Latvia. Like swallows they left the Baltic in great migrations, first during the short period of independence, then shortly before the Second World War.

In the mid-nineteenth century the rise of Riga as an industrial port brought an influx of native Latvians into what was still a predominantly German city. With the encouragement of some progressive Lutheran clergy the long dormant peasantry began to conceive themselves as a nation and the Latvians began to crowd the Germans out of the middle-class professions, amid much the same atmosphere of ethnic tension that exists in Riga today between Latvians and Russians. During the 1850s, Latvians began to outnumber Germans in Riga and there followed a long conflict for control of the city council.

With the outbreak of revolution, many Latvians joined Lenin's Bolsheviks. Among Lenin's personal bodyguard was a group of riflemen who were later immortalised in stone in front of St Peter's church. Many others, however, seized the opportunity provided by the weakness in St Petersburg to proclaim an independent state. Either way, the news was bad for the Germans, whose great land holdings were broken up. Many emigrated.

The rump of the Baltic Germans remained until the August of 1939, when Hitler signed away the independence of the Baltic states to the Soviet Union. As part of the arrangement, the German community was evacuated lock, stock and barrel to metropolitan Germany between August and 10 October 1939 when Latvia's brief essay in self-government came to an end.

Today the citizens of Riga require interpreters to understand the magnificent funerary monuments of the old *burgermeisters* of Riga in the Domus and the worn rhyming couplets one finds on street corners and in small squares, such as one I found inscribed over a blind classical doorway behind a row of old merchants' houses in Small Palace Street called 'The three brothers'. It reads: 'Mit Gott geh aus und ein, so wirst du segnet sein' ('With God go out and in, then you will be blessed'). Only in the life of the church and the tradition of choral music do the traditions of the old Baltic Germans continue to breathe.

Bishop Albert's greatest gift to the city of Riga was the foundation of the city's pride and glory, the gothic cathedral known as the 'Doms'. The present Doms contains little of the humble basilica erected by bishop Albert, most of which now dates from the fifteenth and eighteenth centuries. It was a monastic foundation, from which a single cloister survives. The catholic furnishings were removed in 1524.

Riga, along with the other German ports, was swept with reformation fervour in the 1520s, and long after the Germans departed out of Latvia the majority of Latvian Christians remain members of the Lutheran church. The Doms was closed to religious worship under Nikita Khrushchev's anti-religious campaign, but it remains a centre of Latvian choral music, which owes much to German and Lutheran traditions. The Doms's organ is said to be the largest in the world, the present model having been constructed by the house of Walker in Wurttemburg in 1883.

A sequence of stained-glass windows dating from the cathedral's nineteenth-century restoration depicts episodes in the life of the city, as seen from the point of view of the German merchant class. In one is the foundation of the city by Bishop Albert. Martin Luther peers down from another. Another shows the city *burgermeisters* handing over the keys of the city of Riga to a resplendent and silver-armoured King Gustavus Adolphus of Sweden.

Late medieval maps of Riga show four other churches, all of which survive. The most impressive is St Peter's, whose high wooden spire surmounted by Bishop Albert's cockerel is the symbol of the city. Unfortunately the church was almost entirely destroyed in 1941, hence the present naked interior, though the electric lift to the top of the spire affords a delightful view over the city. The town hall square in front of the church was once lined with sixteenth-century merchants' houses, all unfortunately destroyed in the war. The present bare *piazza* is remarkable only for the post-war sculpture of the Red Riflemen, representing the revolutionaries from Riga who acted as Lenin's personal bodyguard.

Of the two churches behind St Peter's, only St John's still functions as a Lutheran church, the neighbouring church of St George, once the chapel of the Order of the Knights of St George, having fallen into dereliction. St John's was originally the chapel of a nearby Dominican monastery and was rebuilt in a mannerist style in the sixteenth century. The church is always open in the day during summer for organ recitals, though unfortunately many of the younger citizens of Riga make use of this hospitality for an afternoon kip.

St Jacob's church, which is now used by Roman catholics, also owes its origins to the industrious Bishop Albert, though the present structure dates from the sixteenth century. There is a famous legend concerning its bells, or rather lack of bells. The legend suggests that the bells of this particular church enjoyed unusual powers to detect the state of the souls of those who passed by. They rang out unaided whenever an unfaithful spouse went down the nearby street. One day the mayor processed in great state past the church and to his humiliation the bells rang out with particular verve and aplomb. The angry mayor ordered the bells to be thrown into the river Daugava and the church was silenced in its witness!

There is a café society of sorts in Riga, though it languishes. This is not on account of any lack of interest from the citizens of Riga, but because the tyrannical waiters who man the doors, cafés and restaurants in Riga are rigidly divided in a most unmarxist manner into 'categories'. 'Category two' presented no problems about entrance, but they looked unappetising and mean-spirited. I felt certain that the German ladies of pre-war Riga would have been appalled to discover what had happened to the cosy corners where they once had their mid-morning *kaffee und kuchen*.

The 'category one' establishments were a great improvement, but the waiters operated a pernicious lock-and-chain policy on the door that made it almost impossible to enter unless I was willing to sacrifice an entire morning just for a cup of coffee. The Latvians were clearly determined not to follow the Polish road and spread their butter too thinly on the bread by having a great many cafés which contained nothing. Nor will the Latvians be cheated of their hours of queuing only to have to share a table. I once waited several hours to get into a restaurant only to find a half dozen people inside. Each one was occupying an entire table and they were all taking as long as possible to drink their cups of coffee. The only person who was enraged about this was me. The rest of the silent shuffling queue seemed to find this perfectly acceptable behaviour.

The Latvians and Lithuanians have a penchant for situating their better restaurants in underground cellars decorated in a fake old-world style, with open brickwork and shields hanging on the walls. But whereas the Lithuanians had the where withall to furnish the Senasys Rusys in Vilnius with foreign menus, I did not find one restaurant in Riga in which the menu was printed in any other language than Latvian or Russian.

Most of the time I sidestepped this difficulty by the vulgar habit of escorting the waiter to another table and jabbing at whatever delicacy had taken my fancy. Sometimes I was reduced to the desperate expediency of imitating chickens, cows or pigs to order the main course. This tactic did not, of course, allow me to order fish or cake.

This did not save me in the Café Ridzene beside St John's church. This charming café attracted my attention because it was not in a cellar and because I discovered what I believe is the only café in Riga with a string quartet.

A mere half hour of stamping my feet and smoking cigarettes outside brought me to a seat equipped with a menu written in Latvian and Russian. I looked round in the hope of catching sight of a plate of beef or pork, but I had arrived so early that no one was eating. At the sight of all these well dressed young Latvians with their elegant girl friends my courage failed. How could I interrupt a string quartet by oinking or doing my chicken impressions? I pointed meekly at the indecipherable Cyrillic of the menu and prayed it was chicken, or at least that it wasn't brains. The waitress looked slightly puzzled and disappeared.

She returned with a piece of cake. I sighed, began eating the cake, and pointed at another item in a different section. It was in the middle of the menu so I was sure it was a main course. The waitress raised her eyes and disappeared.

She returned with a plate of icecream. I began eating the icecream alongside the cake and grimly pointed at yet another item, which turned out to be pork and chips. I cannot say I enjoyed eating a three-course meal in reverse order, and vowed never to make such an expedition again without a Russian dictionary.

I met my young friend as arranged in the foyer of my hotel for a trip to the outdoor folk museum. She wanted to travel by bus to the museum, but I insisted on us going by taxi. She agreed reluctantly. We flagged a cab down and sped through the streets.

'How many Russians are there in Riga?' I asked, still thinking about the red flowers and poems strewn over the Freedom Memorial. She shook her head silently and pointed at the taxi driver. 'Russian,' she whispered. I felt suddenly appalled that she was really frightened of speaking her mind in a cab in case the driver overheard her.

'Don't ever have a conversation like that in a taxi,' she said as we got out. 'Most of the taxi-drivers are Russian and some of them have tapes.' Whether the taxi-drivers of Riga really carried round cassettes with which to record the conversations in the back or not, it seemed terribly sad that my young friend lived with the assumption.

'Relations between Russians and Latvians are very bad in Riga right now. There are fights in the street between Latvian and Russian boys. The people are very angry that whenever they build a new factory in Latvia they always bring in Russians to live in Latvia. But I think the Russians are worried. I overheard two women on the tram yesterday saying they thought the Russians might have to leave Latvia. I hope so.'

I do not normally like museums very much, but my friend was so interested in the open-air museum that it was hard not to fall in with her enthusiasm. The museum was set in a large area of woodland in which wooden houses and churches had been assembled from various provinces in the Latvian countryside. Most of the houses had been brought to Riga in the 1920s, just after the proclamation of Latvian independence, when interest in Latvian folk culture was at its height. With the passing of the decades, they looked as if they had grown into their surroundings, so the museum looked rather like an authentic village.

There were women in Latvian national dress sitting on the porches of several of the huts. 'Some of these women are intellectuals who know a lot about our culture,' my companion informed me as we strode into one hut. 'Until a year ago they were not allowed to talk to visitors about it. Now they can.'

The woman in peasant dress was much pleased by our interest and began to demonstrate the various ways in which peasant women from different regions of Latvia wore their headdresses. 'This colour was only permitted for virgins,' whispered my companion. 'But that one was only for widows.'

The sun was setting as we left the hut. 'I feel like Robinson Crusoe looking for a hut in which to live,' my friend said as we strode over the grassy knolls back towards the bus station. I asked for her address, which broke the spell immediately. 'I don't think that would be a good idea,' she said, before boarding the bus and stiffly waving me goodbye.

BALTIC

Leningrad

THE WOMAN in charge of our carriage had a cigarette in her mouth and was stoking a boiler. 'Tea?' she offered brightly. She prodded the ashes of the boiler rather gingerly with a poker and lit another cigarette as the boiler hissed and bubbled into life. It was morning and we were approaching the great imperial city of Leningrad, the other end of an axis that began in Berlin. From the window of the train I could see a row of modern tower blocks and industrial plant which sprawled for miles without any trace of planning. I felt I was crossing the last wall and awaited revelation.

When the boiler began to bubble and hiss to the carriage attendant's satisfaction she poured the water into a row of old, battered, silver-plated mugs. These she carried carefully one by one down the corridor into the various compartments, obviously unwilling to risk using a tray in case they were dropped. By the time she reached my cabin at the end of the corridor, the water was quite cold and the sugar lumps sat obstinately in the bottom of the mug. But I appreciated her kindly manner.

The train drew in at the Finland Station, where Lenin had staged his triumphant return to the Russian capital in order to oversee the Bolshevik Revolution. A faithful Intourist official was waiting on the platform. But this was Leningrad and, like any great city, she feels no need to woo visitors by being specially ingratiating, so to my great disappointment the Intourist official did no more than cast me a casual glance, tick my name off a list and escort me into a waiting taxi. 'Olgino,' he shouted through the window.

The taxi sped through the centre of Leningrad along embankments lapped by the cold waters of the Neva. We bounced over bridges from which I could see the golden needle spire of the St Peter and St Paul fortress, drove on through nineteenth-century suburbs, my heart now sinking in exact proportion to the distance we were travelling from the centre of the city, over another bridge and out into a miserable scrubland that was neither town nor country, only verges and huts.

In the back of the taxi, I seethed impotently, feeling that it was monstrous of Intourist to have booked me in to a hotel so far from civilisation. The taxi-driver pressed the accelerator when we reached the motorway and as we passed a large sign indicating that we had crossed the city boundary, my anger began to melt into raw panic.

A few yards beyond the city boundary, however, the taxi swerved off the road into what ressembled a large petrol station. The taxi stopped and I stared gloomily at the drizzle outside. I expected the taxi-driver to get out and fill up the petrol tank, instead of which he sat muttering impatiently in the front seat. I couldn't imagine what he wanted me to do, unless it was to man the petrol pumps myself, but then he loudly announced the word 'Olgino!'

A long cold look through the half-light revealed only petrol pumps in front of a rambling one-storey portacabin. Was it possible that this encampment set in a wasteland was my future residence? The taxi-driver jumped out of the car and pitched my suitcase out of the door into a waiting puddle. Evidently it was more than possible. It was a fact. As I approached the 'hotel', I could make out two or three long faces pressed against the steamed-up windows. Feeling like Jane Eyre on arrival at Lowood school I propelled myself unwillingly through the glass door into a draughty hall.

'What a dump,' came the broad American voice of a tough-looking lady who was standing at the reception desk, suitcase in hand and looking round in amazement. 'Where the hell *are* we?' she rounded angrily on her husband. She asked me how long it took to get to the centre of the city, having explained that she had fallen asleep in the taxi. 'About three quarters of an hour if you're lucky,' I answered shamefacedly. 'Whaat?' she said accusingly. I felt that she held me partly responsible for this calamitous state of affairs.

Apart from the American lady, the hotel appeared almost deserted. It obviously functioned on summer trade and with the onset of blustering autumn winds and rains was left to a motley collection of waifs, strays and birds of passage like myself. I was left to wander the draughty corridors in the company of a few other pieces of human driftwood, of whom the most ubiquitous were a hairdresser from Riga and a blond youth from Estonia called Ivan. The hairdresser from Riga did not make exciting company as my knowledge of Latvian was insufficient to bring our long but desultory chats in the gloomy bar to life. I soon gathered, however, that she had entirely run out money and was desperately casting round for someone who would pay for her train ticket back to Riga. As I was foolish enough to tell her that I had recently been in Riga, this information immediately awoke in her mind the entirely false expectation that that was where I was intending to return. In the breakfast room she would hover round my table each morning with a hang-dog expression on her face, as though she suspected that I was secretly planning to return to Riga without her.

Ivan was a male prostitute. Or maybe he just had a funny conversational manner, because he would always end the most perfunctory exchanges about the weather, the price of fish or the number of cafés in Tallinn by fishing a key-ring out of his pocket, swinging it round his finger and huskily murmuring the phrase, 'I am in room 47. Come anytime.' The more one spoke to him the more emphatic he was on this point, until after three beers he began saying, 'Come *any* time' with such grim determination that I felt obliged to arrange a provisional appointment in Room 47 at the very least. I must admit that as I nursed a black coffee and a cigarette in the dim light of the bar, whilst rain drizzled down the window panes, the secret fleshpots of 'room 47' worked upon my imagination to such an extent that I resolved on keeping my appointment. In the event I was sorely disappointed to discover on Wednesday at three o'clock, the time we had arranged to meet, that 'room 47' was already occupied and in business when I arrived.

Ivan was rather well off so both the hairdresser and I forgave these minor breaches of promise, as Ivan liked to advertise his wealth by supplying both the hairdresser and myself with American cigarettes as well as paying a £10 bill daily for our taxi rides into the centre of Leningrad.

Ivan was almost supernaturally ubiquitous. Sometimes I went for drinks in the Hotel Moscow for a change of atmosphere. Ivan was always there, hunched over the bar, sipping a Pina Colada and scanning the scene with the predatory attention of a cormorant. I visited the still more exclusive bar in the Hotel Pribaltiskija, from which Soviet citizens were theoretically excluded, as it dealt exclusively in hard currency. Ivan was there too, of course, again propped up on a bar-stool and casting round the room with his loaded eyes. It faintly irritated me that Ivan was never half as suprised to see me as I was to see him. He appeared to have rooms everywhere as well and when I stopped for a brief, gawky chat, he terminated the conversation with the laconic comment: 'I am in room 805. Come anytime.'

There were more signs of life at the Hotel Olgino in the caravans that were parked in the square outside. These caravans mostly belonged to Finns who had come to Leningrad for the purpose of drinking as much alcohol as they could without killing themselves, before returning stupefied to the badlands of the Arctic Circle. One of these Finnish couples invited me for drinks in their snug, bottle-lined hideout, along with the Latvian hairdresser and a few other wretches they had spied shuffling miserably round the petrol pumps in the forecourt of the hotel. Once inside their caravan I found a bright-eyed, bushy-tailed young Russian couple in their twenties who were, however, in a savagely bad mood for reasons none of us could establish. There was a gun-toting policeman who kept nervously peering out of the door to see if any of his superiors knew where he was. We all gave up with the Latvian hairdresser, as she insisted on bringing the most unlikely subjects round to the price of train tickets to Riga. The policeman appeared torn between pride in his job and a wish to ingratiate himself with the predominantly western atmosphere in the caravan. 'I *am* a policeman,' he said, as if the fact of his uniform and gun might have escaped us, but he managed to invest this statement with a feeling that such superficial judgments were illusory, if not down-right mistaken. '... but I also play jazz, you know, dum, diddle dee.' He stood up and vanished out of the door at midnight, like Cinderella, and then returned a little while later triumphantly brandishing a handful of six fresh crayfish. We all wondered where he had got them.

The Finnish couple became terribly drunk. They began to hurl abuse at each other, not in Finnish, however, but in English. Even in their cups they retained their international perspectives.

'Hey, you. Fat woman. Why you fat? Ha!'

'Who is fat?'

'You fat.'

'Me fat? You are fat and useless man.'

And so it continued until they decided to abuse the Russian policemen instead about the province of Karelia which, as we all discovered in some detail, had been involuntarily detatched by Stalin from Finland after the Winter War of 1940.

'You give us back Karelia,' the Finnish woman shouted threateningly. The Russian policeman grinned. He was evidently being asked to nip out of the caravan and produce Karelia with the same ease that he had procured the handful of fresh crayfish.

The Russian couple, however, became even more horribly drunk than the Finns. 'You are English?' the young man kept on asking. No matter how many times I answered 'yes, that's right' he always came right back with the same question five minutes later. Shortly after eating the crayfish his wife became quite insensible and began to snore gently in the corner. The young Russian looked carefully at his sleeping spouse, grabbed my hand and, with a cracked grin on his face that was decidedly off-putting, began to mobilise his lips into mouthing something some new and untried phrase in English. We all stopped talking and looked and waited to be disappointed with yet another round of 'You are English?' The Russian giggled wildly and with immense effort announced instead, in the full earshot of the assembled company of the caravan, 'Let's fuck.'

This statement descended on to our dulled ears, bleary eyes and stupefied brains like a large bucket of extremely cold water. There was a ghastly silence, punctuated by one last strangulated giggle from the Russian.

'What he say?' asked his wife, blinking her eyes and waking up with a yawn. The Finn grinned broadly, but his wife gave me a look of extreme malevolence, having evidently concluded that the fault was entirely mine. 'You ... disgusting ... *pig!*' she spluttered. The effort of speaking English was almost too much given the quantity of whisky swimming around her brain, but she was determined to get it all of her chest. 'You filthy English ...' Her finger pointed right at my nose. '*You* want to do ... your ... disgusting ... things ... in *my* caravan?'

Sunday morning was bright, vividly so after the liquid evening that preceded it. Ivan was nowhere to be seen, so I decided therefore to go into town by tram. As it was a Sunday, I decided it was also time for church. I took the bus to the edge of the city from where I boarded the first tram. The tram was full but I managed to find one vacant seat opposite a young man who appeared to be asleep, until he began to emit grunts and gasps of a most distressing character. I looked round uncomfortably in the vague expectation of some moral support from my fellow passengers in the shape of a wink, or a weary shake of the head, but the only person who was interested in these painful noises was me, even when, after emitting a hoarse snort, an immense snort, an immense globule of green phlegm that was the size of a golf ball burst out of the man's nose and ran down his jacket. Still he did not stir.

It was difficult to project my thoughts forward with much enthusiasm to the coming celebration of the Lord's own service at the Lord's own board with this grim reminder of the fallibility of human nature right in front of my eyes. I tried burying my concentration in a book of Stevie Smith's poems, but I opened it most unfortunately to a poem entitled 'To a dead vole' and which began 'Now vole art dead and done is all thy bleeding', which for some reason turned my thoughts right back to the man in front of me even more, especially as he was unmistakably beginning to tip gently forward off his seat on account of the swaying movement of the tram.

With a final shudder and a swerve the tram burst out from the blackened buildings of the backstreets of Leningrad on to the sun-lit river frontage of the Neva, revealing in all its unexpected glory a panorama of golden cupolets and spires. 'What has Berlin, or Prague got to compare with this?' I exclaimed to myself, somewhat dutifully, as I simultaneously calculated that within a few seconds my lap was about to receive the head of the man opposite me, golf ball of viscous phlegm included. I should have got up and forced my way past the indifferent throng of passengers holding on to the leather straps on the roof of the tram, but the tram jerked and the man shot forward from his seat before I had to rise. Instead of landing on my lap, however, his head shot directly through my legs like a well aimed goal and lodged firmly between the metal bars of my seat. We both stayed stock still after this, I shocked, he entirely unconscious, and there we remained like a piece of modern sculpture, until I got off the tram outside the St Peter and St Paul fortress.

Leningrad is a young city, far younger than New York, for example, and the precise date of its foundation is not shrouded in the myths and parables that envelope Riga and Tallinn in a fanciful haze of Baltic mist. The story of the city began precisely on 16 May 1703, when Tsar Peter the Great began building the fortress of St Peter and St Paul a few miles from the mouth of the river Neva on a precious sliver of the Baltic coastline which his victorious armies had just captured from the king of Sweden. The tsar was delighted to have achieved an historic Russian aim of gaining access to a warm, or warmish, water port on the Baltic sea, as the old Russian port of Archangel in the north was frozen for most of the year. Defying the scepticism of his advisers, who expected Sweden to reconquer their lost territory before long, the Tsar celebrated his triumph by promptly erecting a star-shaped bastion in the estuary named after St Peter and St Paul. It cannot have looked altogether magnificent, surrounded by gnats, ducks and a great quantity of mud, but with that presence of mind which is the hallmark of the truly great, the Tsar seems to have envisioned from the start that the desolate expanse before him would one day blossom into the dazzling imperial metropolis of palaces and spires known to us today.

In the middle of the fortress, the Tsar constructed a church, where he would eventually be buried alongside the other Tsars and Tsaritsas who succeeded him on the imperial throne of the Romanovs. This church was Russian orthodox, but in respect of its external appearance it was quite different from the hot little onion-domed churches of Moscow. It might in fact have been a large protestant chapel transplanted from the lands of England or Holland where the young Tsar had wandered during the impressionable and adventurous years of his youth. In its occidental flavour the new church was a foretaste of the character of the city that was to grow up with astonishing speed around the fortress of St Peter and St Paul. For the Tsar gave Russia's celebrated 'window on the west' a German-sounding name to match its western appearance – St Petersburg.

The erection of the fortress of St Peter and St Paul was soon followed by the construction of a shipyard on the sight of the present Admiralty, which building is still surmounted by a tall ship's mast in acknowledgment of its origins. The Tsar built his city in a spirit that emphatically repudiated the orthodox Byzantine traditions which moulded every crevice of Moscow. He appointed as his architects, among others, an Italian, Domenico Trezzini, a German, Andreas Schluter, and a Frenchman, Alexandre Jean Baptiste LeBlond. Previous Tsars, it is true, also employed foreign architects for great building projects in Moscow. Tsar Ivan IV, 'Ivan the Terrible', chose an Italian in the sixteenth century to build St Basil's cathedral in Red Square. But in the case of St Basil's, although the foreign architect drew upon the latest Italian technology, he imbued his creation with a Muscovite flavour by drawing on the examples of the historic monasteries he saw around him. What was novel and even shocking to contemporary Russian eyes about St Petersburg was the manner in which Tsar Peter freed his protégées to throw off the precedents of Russian ecclesiastical history altogether and build a city on Russian soil that was thoroughly western and secular in mind and body. It was, indeed, in no way different from the great royal capitals of western Europe which had grown up under very different cultural and political conditions in a process lasting a thousand years or so. This tiresome civic puberty the Tsar decided to bypass with a stroke of the pen, or, as regrettably was the case, with the stroke of the lash. The architects rigidly adhered to an austere baroque style which was wholly uninfluenced by Byzantium or orthodoxy and which rejected the rhythm and soul of Russian history even more starkly than did the Soviet revolutionaries of a later era. They laid down a great royal boulevard named the Nevsky Prospekt, canals which resembled those in Amsterdam, and gardens which were inspired by the Palace of Versailles.

The Tsar cooly defied nature by erecting a city in the unhealthily mosquito-infested marshes of the Neva. Now he defied slothful human nature as well by uprooting the Russian nobility from their comfortable Moscow palaces and replanting them like roses in his embryonic capital. The royal princesses, the Tsaritsa and the Tsarevnas, were induced to spend part of the year in gerry-built draughty new residences in St Petersburg, where it was often difficult to buy any food except at the most prohibitive prices. There they shed their eastern veils and donned the dress of eighteenth-century European ladies, sometimes with disconcerting results. More than one visitor commented on the uncomfortable mixture of European court dress and blackened teeth, which in old Muscovy had been a sign of eminent social status and which some Russian noble ladies were reluctant to discard. From 1708 a portion of the Russian nobility were ordered to reside in St Petersburg as well. The Tsar regulated the appearance of his new city to a degree that would have seemed extraordinary in England, where the London merchants had old and established vested interests of their own with which to thwart the many plans for reordering the appearance the English capital put forward by the frustrated English kings. For the Russian Tsar, like most of his successors down to the time of the revolution of 1917, wished to have the best of both worlds, the trappings of western civilisation on the one hand with an unreconstructed oriental despotism on the other. Having ordered his boyars to change their physical appearance by cutting off their beards, Tsar Peter now commanded them to live in a style he considered appropriate by building houses in the city that were made of stone and which were to be no less than two storeys high.

Leaving the fortress of St Peter and Paul, I crossed over the river Neva to the square outside the Hermitage. 'Palace Square', as it used to be known, was now lined with stalls selling pastries to the Sunday-morning strollers. There are a great many soldiers and sailors on the streets of Leningrad and in the queue for pastries was a young man who was off to sign up for his compulsory military service. The Russians are sometimes portrayed by casual observers as fanatical patriots who are always ready and willing to fight and, indeed, die for their motherland. Why this should be so I cannot understand as I have never come across any Russians who were perceptibly more enthusiastic about fighting than the citizens of any other country. This young man, indeed, was bitter about the prospect of his impending departure for Cuba. 'It's a good thing military service is compulsory in the USSR,' he said sarcastically, 'or the Red Army would have about ten soldiers.'

In Palace Square one Sunday morning in January 1905, a momentous demonstration heralded the end of the era that began when Tsar Peter built his marshland fortress on the banks of the Neva. A remarkably dashing-looking priest named Father Georgi Gapon, who in spite of having been recruited by the Tsar's secret police seemed genuinely committed to those he was employed to spy on, led a great deputation of workers from the factories of St Petersburg to the Winter Palace, where he intended to convey their grievances in a petition to the 'Little Father', as the then Tsar Nicholas II optimistically styled himself.

The petition was touchingly expressive of the hopes many ordinary people still vested in the Romanov dynasty to close the appalling cleavage in Russian society between the extravagant plutocracy and the exploited mass of workers and peasants. It was the last time that the toiling masses would address the Romanovs with the old humility of the *muzhiks* before their anointed Lord. Nor would the workers of St Petersburg ever again march to the Tsar's palace under the banners of the orthodox church.

The petition began: 'Sire, we the working men and inhabitants of St Petersburg, our wives, our children and old parents have come to you to seek truth, justice and protection ... that is why we have come to the walls of your palace ... tear down the wall between yourself and your people and let them rule together with you. ... Examine our requests dispassionately and carefully: they are not evil in intent, but meant to help us and You.'

Under Father Gapon's leadership, the workers assembled at five points in the city, marshalled by other clergy bearing icons and portraits of the Tsar and Tsaritsa. In a bucolic and optimistic mood they marched to the Winter Palace.

At the tremendous Narva Arch, which was built to commemorate the triumph of the Russian army over Napoleon, the crowd was met by mounted police who at once began to fire on the crowd. Father Gapon, confused no doubt by a mixture of loyalties, promptly dropped his icons and fled. But in the atmosphere of disorder, many of the demonstrators determined on pressing on towards the palace in spite of the bullets which now rained freely over their heads. The official account was that 130 people were killed in the resulting mayhem, though others estimated the number of casualties at several thousand.

'Bloody Sunday', as it came to be called, was an inexcusable disaster. The Tsar might well have appeared on horseback, splendid and gracious, surrounded by all the trappings of imperial power, before his grubby people. There he might have nobly received the humble petition from Father Gapon and announced some vague but plausible-sounding reform. It was a superb theatrical opportunity for a monarch with even a modicum of intelligence and bravery to grasp the horns of revolutionary fervour and bear them triumphantly off to the Winter Palace. Even in the Russian court, enveloped as it was in a fog of decayed and fatalistic mysticism, there was no shortage of statesmen with enough common sense left to see that the contemporary intolerable conditions of life for the ordinary people had to be rectified if the dynasty was to survive without a terrible reckoning. Amongst them was Count Witte, the future prime minister, who noted after 'bloody Sunday' that 'one bullet whizzed past my head. Another killed the porter at the Alexander Lyceum. I do not know whether the same thing happened everywhere, but on the Troitsky Bridge the troops fired rashly and without rhyme or reason. There were hundreds of casualties ... and the revolutionaries triumphed; the workmen were completely alienated from the Tsar and his government.'

The count's words were accurate, for on 26 October 1905 the St Petersburg Soviet was formed. This body expressed itself on the subject of Tsardom in a very different language from that employed by Father Gapon, which is not altogether surprising because among the leading orators in the Soviet was Leon Trotsky. The January demonstration and the October Soviet seem to belong together on the dividing line of Russian history, for one was the last dispensation of the Old Testament and the other the first chapter of the New.

The faint hopes that I entertained of 'popping into the nearest church' in Leningrad were soon disappointed. In Vilnius and Riga, although the cathedrals were secularised during the Khrushchev era, there still remain a goodly number of functioning churches, for the Baltic states missed out on the great anti-religious campaigns of the late 1920s and 1930s. Religion remains a visible factor in the daily life of these small cities and during my stay in each of them I frequently saw vested clergymen in the streets going about their pastoral business.

In Russia proper the role of the church is far more circumscribed and I knew that in Leningrad I would find that the largest churches had been closed for religious worship. Nevertheless the sheer quantity of cathedrals in Leningrad made me think that scenes of clerical life would not be hard to find.

The great cathedral of St Isaac beside the Admiralty is now a museum. It is an emblem of St Petersburg's western perspectives that owes little to native Russian or orthodox traditions. It would look just as suitable in Paris or London. St Isaac's cathedral was constructed between 1818 and 1858 to the design of a Frenchman, Augustine Monterrand. Many of the five hundred or so sculptures were by the Italian, Vitali. Monterrand died shortly after the cathedral was consecrated in 1858 and as he was French and Roman catholic he was denied his wish to be buried in his monumental construction.

The secularisation of St Isaac's cathedral into a museum does not seem altogether inappropriate. The Italianate ambiance of the cathedral with its triumphal arcades borrows too obviously off the alien aspirations of the catholic and Latin churches of the west to provide a suitable vehicle with which to convey the intimate mysteries of the orthodox faith. The great bronze doors and the vast colonnades of the interior, moreover, fashioned from sixteen different kinds of marble, convey nothing more 'religious' than a kind of awe for the brazen pomp of the Romanov dynasty in commemorating their long Pharaonic rule over all the Russias.

The cathedral of Our Lady of Kazan on the Nevsky Prospekt is of a similar genre. From the outside it recalls the façade of the British Museum and it did not surprise me at all that it was now a Museum of Atheism. Museums of atheism enjoy a notorious reputation in the west and do not even enjoy much esteem nowadays in the USSR. This is principally because they are mostly situated in former churches, which, understandably, seems an unpleasant parody of the building's original function. Museums of atheism symbolise the unbalanced status of religion in the USSR, under whose constitution believers enjoy only the freedom to hold their beliefs, whereas atheists enjoy the crucial extra freedom to publicly promote theirs. The rationale behind museums of atheism, however, is reasonable enough. There is a kind of justice in the notion that organisations like the church, which insist that they hold almost a monopoly on virtue, should be counterbalanced by a parallel organisation whose function is to criticise those claims. Museums of atheism could be kin to a kind of 'Her Majesty's loyal opposition', with a laudable function of keeping the church on its toes.

The Museum of Atheism in Leningrad was fearfully disappointing in this respect. It neither provoked one's indignation by being outrageous nor engaged one's sympathies by providing objects of interest. I had expected posters and photographs which grossly caricatured the church's apostolic claims and which portrayed immensely overweight metropolitans stuffing themselves with caviar and lobster whilst the peasants rotted in their huts. I searched in vain for a catalogue of sensational scandals involving clerics, preferably with a translation into English. Instead Leningrad's Museum of Atheism seemed to have entirely lost its nerve and was given over to an anodyne representation of 'comparative religions' with nick-nacks belonging to various faiths mindlessly strewn about the place with no imagination whatsoever. Here was a medieval chasuble, there was an African tribal mask, in the far corner a stone bug from Egypt. It was all very dispiriting as one felt one could have done so much better. None of these objects conveyed any particular message, atheist or otherwise, and they would all evidently have made a great deal more sense had they been left in the places of worship for which they were designed.

The courtyard outside the cathedral of Our Lady of Kazan is a well known gathering place for the rebellious and politically minded youth of the city. As I left the cathedral I was caught up in a crowd of chanting demonstrators who had gathered in the square. The core of the disturbance was a couple of youths who were shouting '*glasnost* now'. It was not a novel statement of conviction, but a people as short of entertainment as the Russians will cluster around anyone doing something vaguely unusual in public, whether it's someone playing bagpipes or a couple of youths shouting political slogans. So the sight of a these youthful demonstrators choked the square with frantically curious spectators within seconds, all of them pushing and straining forward good-naturedly to find out the source of this exciting disturbance.

'Fascists!' declared an angry old man next to me as the police arrived and bundled the protesting students into a van. His words were clearly directed at the demonstrators rather than the police. 'They are not fascists,' shouted back a tall red-haired student who was wearing an Elvis Presley badge. The student caught sight of my camera and urged me to take a picture of the policemen whilst they struggled to get the last of the students into the van. 'You don't have to worry about a thing if you're from the west,' he assured me. 'They won't touch you.'

I wasn't so sure about this. Reluctantly fingering the camera, I took a picture from as far away as possible. 'Are you sure you got close enough for a newspaper picture?' said the student anxiously. I muttered something about zoom lenses and hoped that he did not know much about cameras. The student introduced himself as Anton, a trainee dentist. He told me that he had also had a number of confrontations with the police. These were not on account of having shouted *glasnost*, however, but through illegally entering foreign-currency bars in the international hotels under the pretence that he was a tourist from Australia.

And so I proceeded like Bunyan's pilgrim on my way to church, now suspecting that there was no functioning cathedral in the city at all, but merely some dismal structure like the Hotel Olgino somewhere out in the scrublands. I called in at the Trinity cathedral, a nineteenth-century building with startling azure blue domes. It looked hopeful as it was out of the city centre and of no special architectural significance. But again it was boarded up and obviously deserted.

Opposite the Trinity cathedral was a small café that was infested with flies. I bought a black coffee and a sad little cake, waved away the flies and examined the map of the city. One cathedral remained on my list, the one called the Nikolskij Sobor or the St Nicholas cathedral.

The approach to the Nikolskij Sobor afforded a dazzling glimpse of golden cupolas sparkling like jewels through the surrounding tree-tops. I was delighted to find a church which looked Russian rather than French, but its exotic beauty made me certain that it must have been converted long ago into another confusing museum of atheism or perhaps a light-bulb factory. At the gates, however, there were a number of old headscarved *babushkas*. And where the *babushkas* clustered I knew I would find an active church.

My first introduction to Russian orthodoxy was the sight of a dead body. An open coffin rested on a bier surrounded by candles in the lower half of the church. Inside the coffin was the corpse of an old lady. A woman in her fifties, who wore a black veil and was possibly the old woman's daughter, was placing flowers in the coffin whilst a priest sung a dirge. Many people were filing past the coffin to look at the corpse, so I felt no embarrassment about doing the same. I peered over the open coffin and looked at the screwed-up face of the old lady, her mouth drawn like purse strings. Her face had a waxen quality, probably from the process of laying out, and it glistened by the light of the surrounding candles. On another bench nearby a half dozen impassive old crones kept watch over the proceedings.

A priest was singing a service on the other side of the church over a row of small cakes made of unleavened bread which had been decorated with ribbons, but my attention was drawn more to the baptism that was taking place in the third corner. I counted at least thirty initiates, ranging from babes in arms to men in their fifties. Several of the adults were parents of the babies that were being baptised and who had obviously decided to take the plunge at the same time. The atmosphere was awkward and embarrassed. The priest and the faithful old woman who accompanied him and who was holding the candles and towels were clearly overwhelmed by the difficulties involved in steering a large congregation of theological illiterates through a complicated service.

Most of the congregation did not know how to cross themselves properly. This may appear a somewhat insignificant point to an Anglo-Saxon observer, but in the orthodox communion, bloodthirsty schisms, castrations and mass self-immolations have occurred over far less. In the seventeenth century an ambitious patriarch of Moscow by the name of Nikon instigated the most devastating conflict the Russian orthodox church has ever experienced merely by altering the number of fingers by which the Russians were to cross themselves, a conflict which has never to date been entirely reconciled. Persecution in the twentieth century may have mellowed the rigour of orthodox intransigence, slightly, on the matter of crossing oneself, and there are even bold schemes to reunite the faithful on the vexed matter of the fingers. The priest in the Nikolskij Sobor, however, eventually became so irritated by the way in which the congregation not only used the wrong number of fingers, but crossed themselves back to front and upside down, that he poked several of them hard in the shoulders to show them in what order they should do it.

The church contained an upper part which I had not seen. I attempted to go upstairs, but a churchwarden shooed me away. 'The metropolitan is coming,' he announced, clearing the pathway from the staircase to the outside door of any curious by-standers. 'And take your hands out of your pockets,' added the woman who was helping the churchwarden with his preparations. I wondered if the metropolitan would emerge to a blast of trumpets, but instead there came the sound of singing, which was not in tune. The doors leading to the upper church burst open and out swept the Metropolitan of Leningrad, a dark and nimble-looking man bearing a pastoral staff, who was immediately followed by a train of plump and supercilious-looking clerics. Singing all the way, this colourful convoy processed at great speed through the church and the courtyard beyond before disappearing into the refectory for lunch.

'I'm not very interested in religion myself,' said a young girl called Olga, a friend of Anton the trainee dentist, as we sat trying to have coffee in the Hotel Europejska, being pestered surrounded by a milling and hissing throng of ne'er-do-wells sidling up and whispering, 'Dollars? Deutschmarks?'

'If you enjoy the sound of the monks singing the liturgy,' Olga continued, 'why don't we all go together to the Alexander Nevsky monastery? It's not far.'

We took a tram down the Nevsky Prospekt and alighted outside a small shop from which there stretched a queue of people several hundred metres long.

'What are they waiting for?' I asked.

'Cakes,' came back the answer.

The rails of the fences along the Nevsky Prospekt, near the statue of the Empress Catherine, were covered with etchings and paintings. Some artists were standing alongside their wares, stamping their feet and clapping their shoulders to keep warm and puffing on home-made cigarettes as they hopefully eyed the boulevard for prospective buyers. Most of the pictures were tasteless reproductions of 'weeping small boy' and such like and were done in shiny lurid colours. Sadly these tired themes attracted by far the most favourable response from the passers by. Sandwiched between all this rubbish, however, was a man with a long beard and a French beret, a veritable artist, who stood beside a delightful collection of minute water colours of small wooden churches which were all evidently his own work.

'You like?' he asked.

'Very much.'

'I am orthodox,' the artist said gravely. He invested such import-ance in this declaration that it was obviously impossible simply to answer, 'Oh I see' or 'How nice for you', and walk away. Indeed I felt duty bound to buy at least two or three of his pictures. As I rummaged around in search of a couple of pictures I particularly liked, I was joined by a German who breathed expressions of wonder-ment and amazement as he searched alongside me. The German's cracked smile, coupled with his nervous affability and palpable anxiousness to please, all betrayed a lifetime of rebuffs in foreign countries. I didn't even have to ask where he was from. 'You're from the DDR,' I simply informed him.

'Why how *did* you know?' he said. 'Here, would you like my address ...?'

We arrived at the monastery gates, opposite the Hotel Moscow, Olga, Anton and me. The pathway up to the monastery was lined with beggars who crossed themselves and murmured prayerful-sounding requests for alms from the concourse of couples walking up and down with their children. When one of the beggars was lucky, he or she bowed low and thanked God with great humility. I was surprised at finding this tableau from Old Holy Russia taking place in the heart of Lenin's city, but Olga assured me that many old people simply did not have enough from their pensions to live on as such pensions depended on completing a full-time job for life. Those who for whatever reason had no such record and who did not have a supportive family turned to begging as the only way of making ends meet.

On a bench outside the monastery we passed an old woman who was describing some passage of her long life with great animation to two attentive youths. Her face was so vivacious in spite of the web of wrinkles that I was convinced she must be relating something very interesting. 'Tell me exactly what she is saying about her life,' I begged Olga. Olga looked at me with surprise. 'Why on earth do you want to know? She's just an old woman!' The idea that this woman who must have lived through the Siege of Leningrad had anything worthwhile to say to the younger generation struck Olga as quite bizarre.

The evening service was in progress in the monastery. It was difficult to get into the church on account of the crowd, but we pushed our way up to the front until we were perched beside the platform upon which stood a great bullfrog of a choirmaster. He looked, and obviously felt, very majestic high up there on his platform, towering over a cluster of headscarved old ladies who made up the choir. These old women he conducted with great authority and he shook his fist furiously when one old lady struck up the wrong note and began singing a completely different refrain from the rest of the group. Anton lost interest in the service and slipped outside to smoke a cigarette. Olga and I remained to the end, mesmerised by the repetitive cadences of the orthodox liturgy.

'Hearing this makes me want to get baptised,' Olga mused as we left the church.

We sat and had coffee in a café near the monastery. I asked Olga if she planned to get married. 'Definitely not,' she said. 'My parents married at the age of eighteen. My mother says only one thing about it: "Don't make the same mistake that I did."' She told me that her mother had only one pleasure in life. 'She dances Russian-style with her arms in the air when she is listening to the music on the radio.'

Public entertainment in Leningrad is concentrated in the big international hotels, where the western tourists can be induced to part with their desperately needed hard currency. These institutions therefore are theoretically off-limits for Soviet citizens, as they are not supposed to be in possession of the magic dollars and deutschmarks. In practice this rule is as dead as a dodo on account of the vast number of people in Leningrad who engage in illicit hard currency transactions with the visiting tourists. Many of the hotel dining rooms in Leningrad which are designed solely for the use of western tourists are in fact wholly occupied night after night by Russians. As for taxi-drivers, it was difficult indeed to get them to accept roubles at all. In the hotels the bar-tenders, the bellhops, the prostitutes and a great many other people from the twilight world spend their days transacting business with foreign tourists. It is impossible to crack down on this trade as the unofficial rate of exchange is at four or five times the official amount, which makes a great incentive for the tourists to break the law. It seems a prohibitive price the Russians pay for access to the glamourous bars of the big hotels, though one only has to taste Russian beer to understand why Russians will pay five times the cost for an export lager. But this currency changes hands many times. The tout who pays five times the official rate for the tourist's pound or dollar will surely be able to sell it again for a far bigger rate in the towns and villages of middle Russia, where the prospect of first-hand contact with western tourists is exceedingly slim.

Olga and Anton 'worked' all the major hotels by posing as Australian or German tourists who had mislaid their passports. Like my former companion in Warsaw, they despised the down-at-heel *fin-de-siècle* glamour of the Hotel Europejska and preferred the airport-lounge modernity of the hotels built in the 1960s and 1970s. The Moscow Hotel outside the Nevsky monastery, with its concrete walkways, spindly tables and flock wallpaper, was one of their favourites. 'Many Russians come here,' Anton informed me seriously, 'because it's so nice inside.'

There we sat on Sunday evening, sunk deep in squelchy chairs that must have been made by the same company which supplied the chairs in the Hotel Victoria in Warsaw. I detested these chairs as I sank so low in the seat that I could barely see over the top and had only to shift a fraction on the rubber seat to emit the most appalling noises. But here we sat, shouting at one another, for the chairs were spread ten feet apart, as Olga delicately sipped her first Bacardi and Anton drank his fourth beer.

I now understood why Anton had so many unfortunate confrontations with the police, as he was unable to resist making a ridiculous *bavardage* with the hotel doorman when he tried to enter the hotel. It was not enough for him to mutter 'Australian tourist' and race inconspicuously through the door into another world, which is all the doorman wanted to know. Instead he slapped the man three times on the back, saying in his thick Russian accent, 'Well done my man. Keep up the good work. Fine weather now in Sydney I hear,' and so on, until, not surprisingly, the doorman became very suspicious indeed and demanded to see Anton's identity card. 'Sorry old fellow, I don't speak a word of Russian,' Anton affably continued, nothing daunted. The doorman by this time was quite certain that he had an illegal Russian student and not a visiting Australian on his hands and he began to shout at Anton in Russian, knowing very well that Anton understood every word that he was saying.

Like my own hotel, the Hotel Moscow was much frequented by the Finnish tourists who had come to drink the town dry. Leningraders like Anton and Olga had no good opinion of these Finns. They disliked them because they had a great deal of money which they only spent on making themselves insensible and because they were apparently immune from any interference from the police whatever their behaviour.

From the deep vantage point of my squelchy chair I discovered how permissive the Soviet officials could be in this respect, for in a nearby chair was a Russian prostitute who was out cold and fast asleep. It was not the prostitute who engaged my attention, however, but an inebriate Finn who had staggered into the bar some minutes after I arrived. He stopped in the middle of the hotel lobby and swayed gently towards the sleeping figure of the woman, who was lying comatose in the chair with her legs slung over the arms. The Finn teetered over to her side and managed to lift her out of the chair and slip himself into it underneath her. With much giggling and passing of knowing winks to the rest of the bar, who sat stock still and quite mortified in their various armchairs, the man began struggling to remove the woman's underpants. He succeeded in wrenching them down between her knees and with all obstacles now removed he placed his hand smartly up her dress. All the time the woman did not so much as stir. She might, in fact, have been dead.

'How disgusting,' said Olga, looking furiously in the other direction, whilst the rest of us stared with a mixture of horror and fascination from deep within our own squelchy chairs. We were all waiting for the long and dreadful arm of Soviet officialdom to move in. But as the offender was a foreigner, nothing happened at all. The bartender merely looked up, peered at the gruesome goings-on with an expression of faint amusement, and then carried on with his crossword.

The Metropolitan of Leningrad arrived in the hotel lobby as the commotion in the squelchy between the sleeping prostitute and the drunken Finn reached its dreadful climax. I was most surprised to see the Metropolitan twice on the same day, but he was immediately recognisable with his black robes, chimney-pot hat and pastoral staff.

'The Metropolitan of Leningrad is here,' I commented a little bleakly.

Anton looked up from his beer. 'Ah you mean the metropol*it*. Metropolit*an* is the name for the underground railway.'

'I hope he doesn't come over here anyway,' I continued.

'He is with a delegation of priests, probably from Finland,' said Olga. The metropolitan appeared fortunately oblivious of what was taking place only a few yards away from him in the deep-set squelchy chair, and was engrossed in animated conversation with the dog-collared clergymen.

'I hope you don't think all Finns are like that,' a Finnish woman shouted from another set of squelchy chairs on the other side of the room, 'because we are not!'

'I am sure you are not,' I shouted back, from deep within my armchair. 'But the Bishop of Leningrad is in this hotel lobby right now.'

The Finnish women looked puzzled by this peculiar answer and looked round. The metropolitan had disappeared with his friends into the restaurant.

The metropolitan was having dinner in the restaurant only a couple of tables away from us. 'Why don't you go over and talk to him?' I suggested to Olga.

'I don't know why you're so interested in him,' she replied. 'These people in the church live a totally separate life from us.' The metropolitan was clinking glasses with one of his Finnish colleagues and murmuring a toast.

I turned my attention to the floor show. A woman in spangles performed a can-can, followed by an ageing rouée who sang romantic ballads in white Cuban heels. Another woman came on and juggled hoops before the stage was given over to the public for dancing. A fat old Finnish man aged about seventy was dancing with two young Russians women in mini-skirts. They escorted him back to his chair when he was out of breath and poured him and themselves some glasses of champagne. Olga wanted to dance as well. I suggested she try out one of the priests as a partner, but she said, 'Russian priests do not dance,' and took the floor alone.

As Olga danced under the spotlight, I sipped my champagne and contemplated my imminent return home in an aeroplane that would whisk me back over the Berlin Wall whence I had come. It had all been very different, but not so different at all once one had acclimatised oneself to the deeper and subtler rhythms that lay close beneath the surface of the water. As Olga danced under the spotlight and the metropolitan raised his glass for yet another toast, I found it increasingly difficult to pinpoint what those differences actually were. Surely there was more to it than communism and cakes without queuing. Did it all boil down to old religious differences between Lutheran Berlin and orthodox Petrograd with catholic Warsaw sandwiched in between? Here in Leningrad, seated at my table and watching the fat old Finn dancing with his twenty-year-old Russian girl friend, there was neither the conclusion nor the revelation I had somehow been expecting since the first moment I crossed the Wall, more a final lifting of the veils of prejudice which divided peoples from other peoples whose religion, culture and expectations were remarkably similar in all the vital respects. Snatches of conversation and snapshots of faces suddenly appeared before me in the shadows from where I was watching the antics on the dance floor. I took a sip of champagne and was back in Berlin, fazed by Mike's dazzling smile as he said, 'You must remember to read the Bible and *Das Kapital*, they're the two most important books in the world.' Another sip and Dagmar and Baronius were sitting like two mice in the auditorium at Auschwitz watching a crackly old film about German atrocities, Andrej was throwing his German dictionary on the floor and laughing in his crowded apartment in Cracow, the flock of jackdaws was rising from the trees in Vilnius and wheeling and soaring above the head of the blonde Intourist guide.

'Very nice. Very poetically put. You almost convinced *me*,' said Dagmar, who had now joined me for a final sip of champagne. 'May I?'

'Of course,' I said, 'Go ahead.'

She fished out a DDR Club cigarette, but I offered her a Marlboro.

'Thank you,' she said. 'What I wanted to say was, since you find it all so romantic, why don't you stay here, I mean not necessarily here in Leningrad, but with any of us, with Baronius and I in Karl Marx Stadt, or with this friend of yours in Cracow, or the Intourist guide in Vilnius whatever her name was? You seem to find it all rather snug. In fact I have a better idea. We could swap lives. You could take over my life in Karl Marx Stadt and I could slip right in where you left off in London, doing whatever it is you did there.

'Don't be so silly. I couldn't even if I wanted to. I can't just drop into Erfurt and take up where someone left off in the middle of a conversation in the Turmschenke restaurant.'

'Then why be so lyrical about it all? You're almost as bad as those people who come over the Berlin Wall for three days and then write about our lives as if it were some big drama in which we all spend our time waiting for the midnight knock on the door from the secret police or praying for a passport to America? You're deliberately distorting reality for the sake of poetic licence. What is all this stuff about "flocks of jackdaws, wheeling and soaring" and me and my husband sitting "like two mice" in the auditorium? He'd be delighted to hear that! You know very well that if you really stepped out of those big hotels you've been staying in and came on down to where we really were, you'd find it wasn't snug at all. Air-raid shelters aren't very snug when you spend your whole life in them, you know. They're just monotonous.'

'I know,' I said apologetically. 'I just wanted to say that before the curtain goes up, before Gorbachev finally lets you all out of your cages and your lives start to merge indistinguishably with ours, that you ought to know that this freedom you want so much isn't quite what you expected. After the first rush of blood to your head, you'll find yourself isolated by your new-found freedom, alienated and fused by the bewildering choices presented to you.' Dagmar was silently shaking her head and slowly disappearing, but I continued nevertheless. 'For goodness' sake don't imagine that what we have over there is "DDR minus the barbed wire". It's not. It's a totally soulless . . .'

She'd gone and I turned to watch Olga still dancing on her own under the spotlight, lost in private reverie. As she began dancing in the Russian style by throwing her hands up into the air and kicking out her heels I tried to recall the first impression of the expedition, the Berlin Wall. But as on that first evening in the east, when I had looked back, as anxious as Lot's wife for the world I had left behind me, my vision was blurred and the Wall hovered nebulous and faint in the mist.

Born in Surrey, England, in 1961, Marcus Tanner was an Anglican seminarian before going on to read history at York University and theology at Cambridge, where, in 1986, he was awarded the Cambridge University Prize for Church History. Mr. Tanner, who has served as an Anglican missionary and teacher in India, is currently the Belgrade correspondent for the London *Independent*.